Chess Rules For Students

Chess Rules For Students is an instructional workbook designed for students just learning the game of chess and for beginning students returning to the game after an absence. Parents unfamiliar with chess will find this booklet a valuable guide to their child's new interest. *Chess Rules For Students* is designed with students, coaches, and parents in mind.

- No previous knowledge of chess is necessary.
- Reading level is appropriate for grade-school use.
- All major rules of chess are covered.
- Each page is in easy-to-use worksheet format.
- Page-by-page activities assess student understanding.
- Activities are comprehensive, yet easy to correct.
- Student-friendly Answer Key makes self-correction fun.

Chess Rules For Students follows the standard chess conventions of placing black pieces at the top of chess diagrams and of capitalizing the names of all chess pieces except pawns. The words *white* and *black* are capitalized only when referring to players.

Field-Tested Portfolio Assessment Activity

Chess Rules For Students has been extensively field-tested with elementary, middle-school and high-school students and at-risk students. *Chess Rules For Students* is an ideal portfolio assessment activity.

Goals and Objectives

Upon completion of this booklet, students will know and be able to explain the major rules of chess. Students will demonstrate comprehension of the rules listed below:

- chessboard design and chess vocabulary
- piece moves and captures
- en passant
- pawn promotion
- checking the King
- castling
- checkmate
- drawn games
- algebraic notation

Student Information

Name: _____ Grade: _____

School: _____

Home Address: _____

Home Phone: _____

CONTENTS

Topic   **Page**

The Board
Square and Colors 6
Ranks, Files, and Diagonals 7
Chess Pieces 8
Starting Position 9

Piece Movement
How the King Moves 10
How the King Captures 11
How the Queen Moves 12
How the Queen Captures 13
How Rooks Move and Capture 14
Practicing Queen and Rook Moves 15
How Bishops Move and Capture 16
How Knights Move and Capture 17
Practicing Bishop and Knight Moves 18
How Pawns Move and Capture 19
En Passant 20
Promoting a Pawn 21
Practicing Pawn Moves 22

Checking
Checking the King 23
Practicing Checking 24
Two Moves a King <u>Cannot</u> Make 25
Two More Moves a King <u>Cannot</u> Make 26
Getting Out of Check 27

Castling
Castling 28
When Can a King Castle? 29

Checkmating
Checkmate 30
Practicing Queen Checkmates 31
Practicing Rook Checkmates 32
Practicing Bishop, Knight, and Pawn Checkmates 33

| Topic | Page |

Draws
Stalemate Draw 34
Other Types of Draws 35
Choosing to Underpromote a Pawn 36

Piece Value
Piece Value 37

Checkmate Challenge
Checkmate Challenge I 38
Checkmate Challenge II 39

Algebraic Notation
Learning Algebraic Notation 40
Recording Chess Moves 41
Capturing, Castling, Checking and Checkmating 42
Avoiding Confusion with Like Pieces 43
King Pawn Opening 44
Queen Pawn Opening 45
Special Recording Symbols 46

Game Rules and Courtesies
Game Rules and Courtesies 47

Answer Key
Answer Key 48

Game Record Sheet
Photocopy Master: Game Record Sheet 55

Squares and Colors

> **Instruction**

A chessboard contains 64 squares. The squares are colored light and dark.
- The light squares (usually white, yellow, or red) are called the **white squares**.
- The dark squares (usually black, green, or brown) are called the **black squares**.

At the beginning of a chess game, the board is set up so that each player, when facing the board, has a white square in the lower right-hand corner of the board.

Player A

The Chessboard

← White square is in lower right-hand corner.

Player B

> **Activity 1**

⇨ a. How many squares are on a chessboard? _____

b. How many squares are along each side of a chessboard? _____

c. At the beginning of a game, what color square (*white* or *black*) should be at the lower right-hand corner of the chessboard? _____

d. At the beginning of a game, what color square (*white* or *black*) should be at the lower left-hand corner of the chessboard? _____

e. Does a chessboard contain more *light* squares, more *dark* squares, or an *equal* number of light and dark squares? _____

Ranks, Files, and Diagonals

Instruction

Chess players use the following words to describe a chessboard:
- **Rank:** Each <u>row</u> of squares (running left to right).
- **File:** Each <u>column</u> of squares (running up and down, or top to bottom).
- **Diagonal:** Each <u>slanted line</u> of same-color squares (crossing the board at a 45-degree angle).

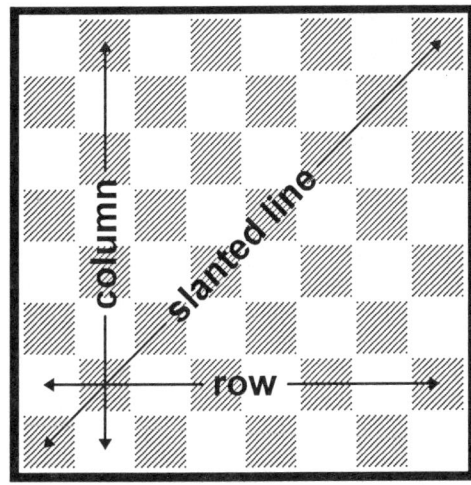

Everyday Vocabulary

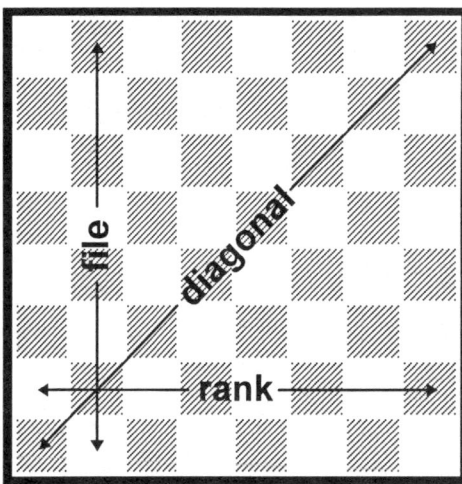

Chess Vocabulary

Activity 2

a. How many ranks does a chessboard contain? _____

b. How many files does a chessboard contain? _____

c. How many squares are on the longest diagonal of a chessboard? _____

d. A *file* runs _____, and a *rank* runs _____.
   (*left to right* or *up and down?*)   (*left to right* or *up and down?*)

e. Match each chess term on the left with its definition on the right.

    Chess Terms   **Definitions**

    ___ **1.** rank   a) slanted line

    ___ **2.** file   b) row

    ___ **3.** diagonal   c) column

Chess Pieces

> **Instruction**

Chess pieces are also colored light and dark, and are called the **white** and **black pieces**. To begin play, each player chooses a color, one player *playing white* and one player *playing black*. Each player sets up the 16 chess pieces of his or her chosen color: 1 King, 1 Queen, 2 Rooks, 2 Bishops, 2 Knights, and 8 pawns. Symbols that are used to represent chess pieces are shown below.

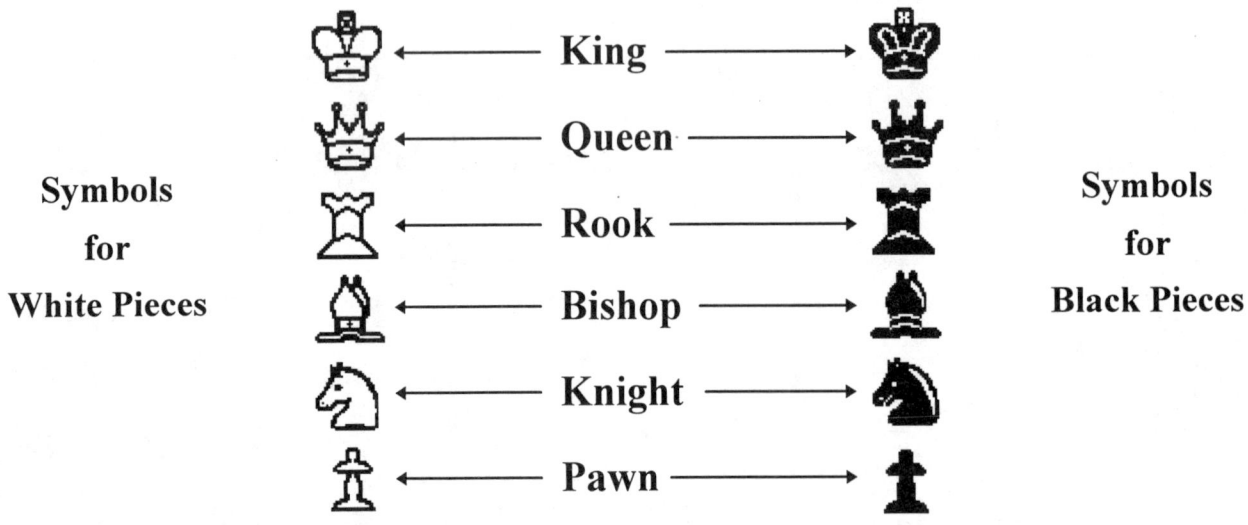

Symbols for White Pieces ← King → **Symbols for Black Pieces**
Queen
Rook
Bishop
Knight
Pawn

> **Activity 3**

a. How many pieces does each player have when play begins? _____

b. How many pieces are on the chessboard when play begins? _____

c. In the diagram below, write the names of the circled pieces.

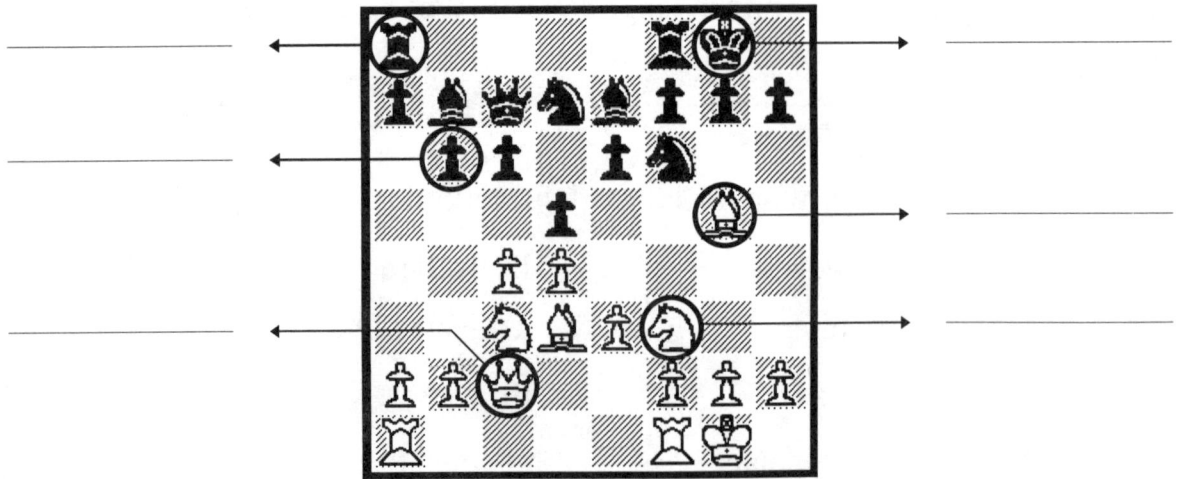

8

Starting Position

> Instruction

The diagram below shows the starting position of both the white pieces and black pieces.

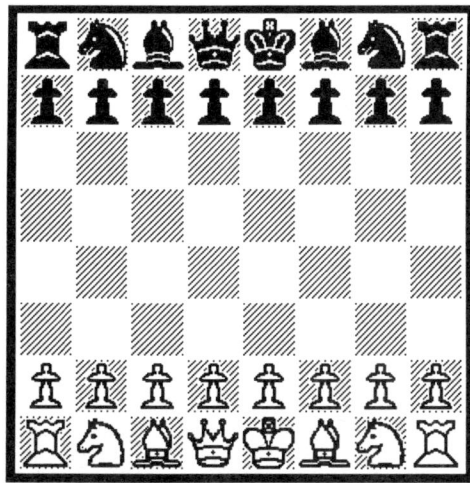

The Chessboard

with Pieces in

the Starting Position

Note: Each Queen stands on her own color. The black Queen stands on black, and the white Queen stands on white.

> Activity 4

a. In the starting position, on what color squares are the Queens placed?

white Queen? _____ black Queen? _____
(*white* or *black*?)   (*white* or *black*?)

b. In the starting position, on what color squares are the Kings placed?

white King? _____ black King? _____
(*white* or *black*?)   (*white* or *black*?)

c. On the diagram at right, show the starting positions of both white and black pieces. Use the following abbreviations: K = King, Q = Queen, R = Rook, B = Bishop, N = Knight, and P = pawn.

d. On your completed diagram, draw a circle around each Queen.

e. On your completed diagram, draw a square around each Rook.

Black Pieces

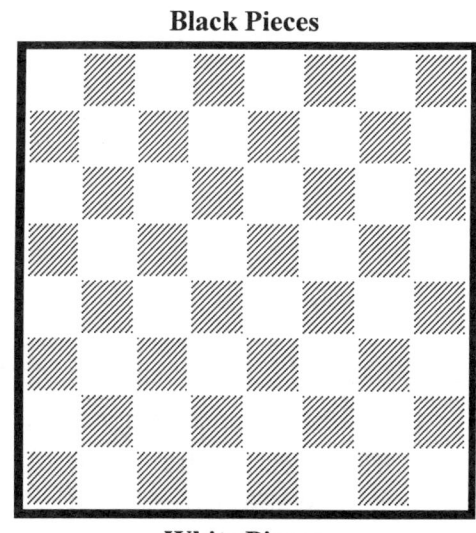

White Pieces

How the King Moves

> **Instruction**

A **move** occurs when a player moves a chess piece from one square to another. Each chess piece moves in its own way. Kings move differently from Queens, which move differently from Rooks, and so on. A **capture** is made when a player moves a piece onto a square occupied by the opponent's piece and then removes the piece from the board. Players may not capture their own pieces.

The King moves one square in any direction. A King can move along a rank, a file, or a diagonal.

In the diagram at right, each King can make its next move to any square next to it (marked with **X**s).

> **Activity 5**

⇨ Use the diagram at right to do the following:

a. Write an **X** on each square to which the black King can move on its next move.

b. Write an **X** on each square to which the white King can move on its next move.

c. What is the least number of moves in which the white King can move to the black square in the lower left-hand corner of the board? _____

d. What is the least number of moves in which the white King can move to the white square in the upper left-hand corner of the board? _____

How the King Captures

Instruction

The King captures by moving onto a square occupied by the opponent's piece and then removing the piece from the board.

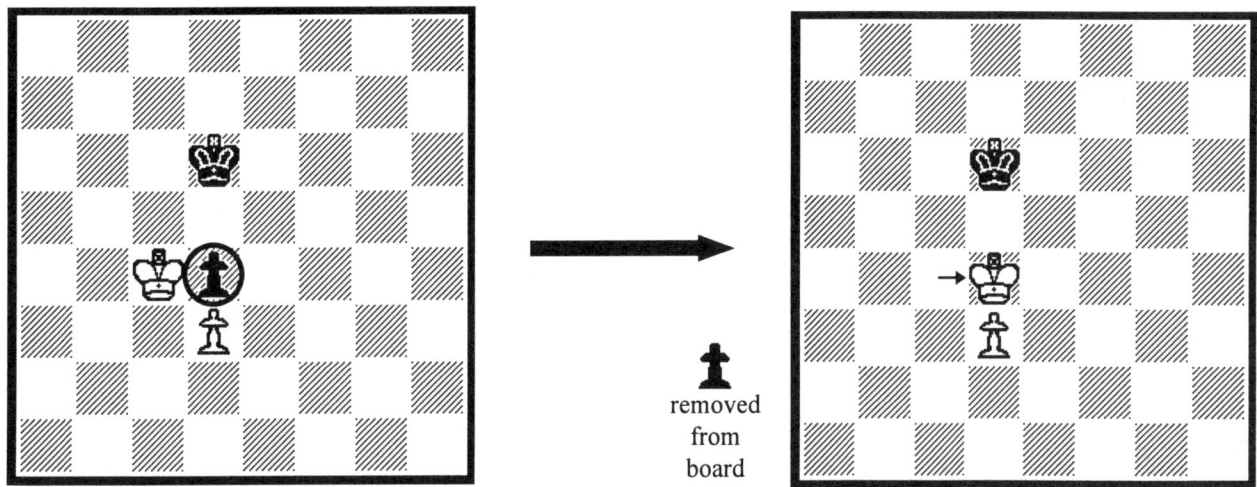

In the diagrams above, the white King captures the black pawn (circled) as shown.

Activity 6

➡ Follow the instructions for each diagram below.

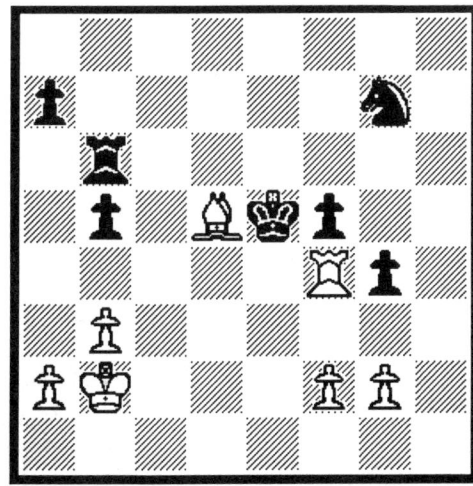   

a. Circle and name the pieces that the black King can capture:

_____ and _____

b. Circle and name the pieces that the white King can capture:

_____ and _____

How the Queen Moves

> **Instruction**

A Queen can move as far as it wants in any direction on a rank, file, or diagonal. The Queen, however, must stop on the square before another piece–unless the Queen plans to capture the piece. The Queen cannot move to squares beyond any piece that blocks the Queen's movement.

The white Queen can move to any square marked with an **X**.

The white Queen can move to any square marked with an **X**, *or* capture the black Bishop (circled). The Queen cannot, however, move to the squares beyond the Bishop or Rook.

> **Activity 7**

⇨ Use the diagram at right to do the following:

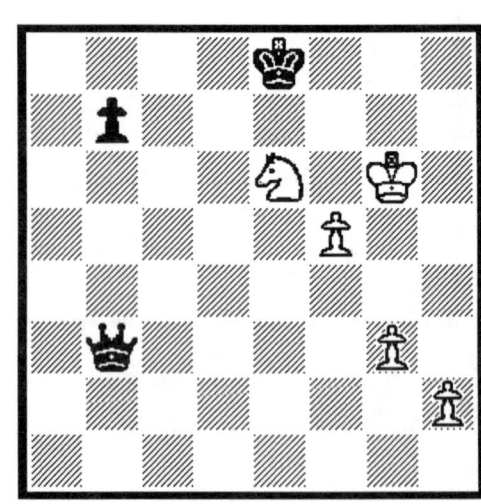

a. Write an **X** on each square to which the black Queen can move, and circle any piece the black Queen can capture.

b. Draw a circle on each square the black Queen cannot reach because its movement is blocked by other pieces.

c. Name the piece that is blocking the Queen's free movement along one of her two diagonals.

12

How the Queen Captures

Instruction

The Queen captures by moving onto a square occupied by the opponent's piece and then removing the piece from the board.

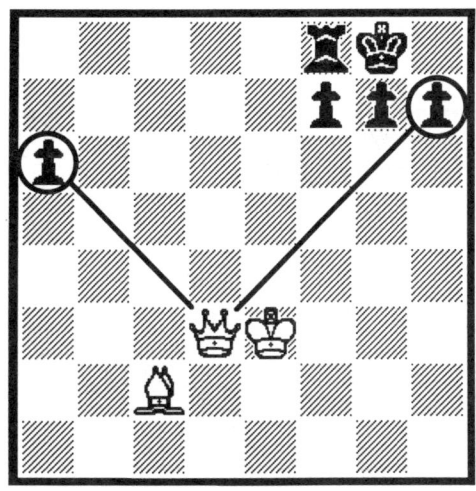 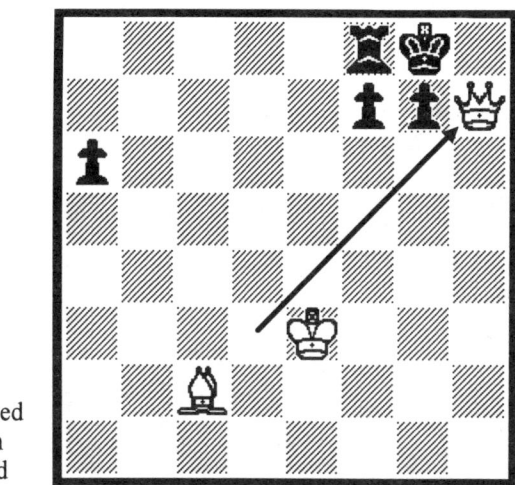

The white Queen can capture either circled black pawn.

The white Queen has captured the pawn on the square indicated by the arrow.

Activity 8

⇨ Follow the instructions for each diagram below.

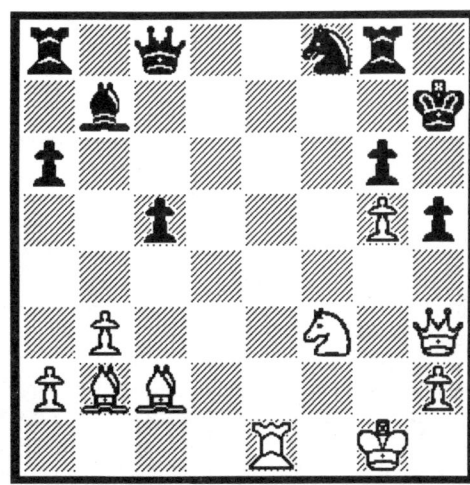 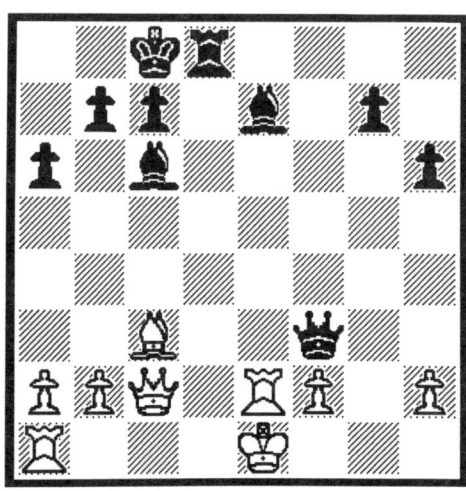

a. Write an **X** on each square to which the white Queen can move, and circle any piece the white Queen can capture.

b. Write an **X** on each square to which the black Queen can move, and circle any piece the black Queen can capture.

How Rooks Move and Capture

| Instruction |

A Rook can move as far as it wants along a rank or a file. It must stop, however, on the square before another piece–unless the Rook plans to capture an opponent's piece. The Rook captures by moving onto a square occupied by the opponent's piece and then removing the piece from the board.

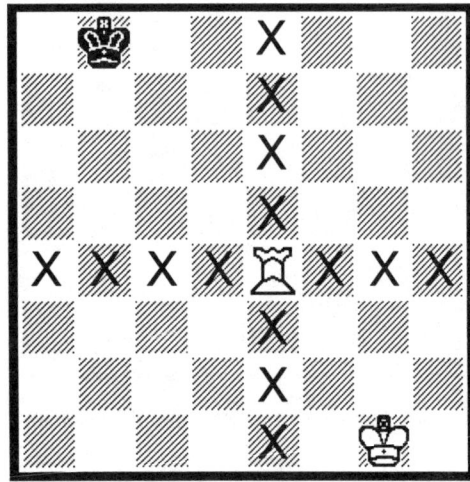

The white Rook can move to any square marked with an **X**.

The white Rook can move to any square marked with an **X**, or capture the black Bishop (circled). The Rook cannot move to the squares beyond the black Bishop or white Knight.

| Activity 9 |

⇨ Use the diagram at right to do the following:

a. Write an **X** on each square to which the white Rook can move, and circle any piece the white Rook can capture.

b. Draw a circle on each square the white Rook cannot reach because its movement is blocked by other pieces.

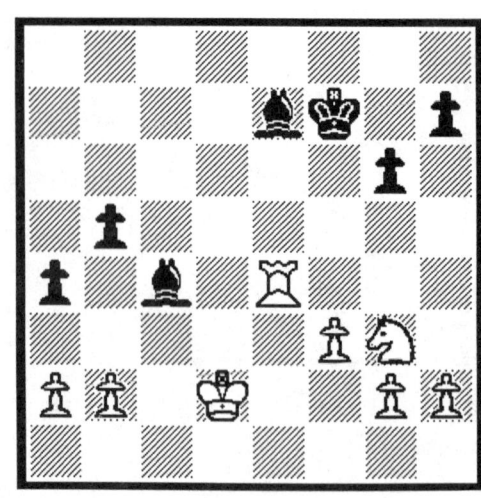

Practicing Queen and Rook Moves

Activity 10

⇨ Follow the instructions for each diagram below.

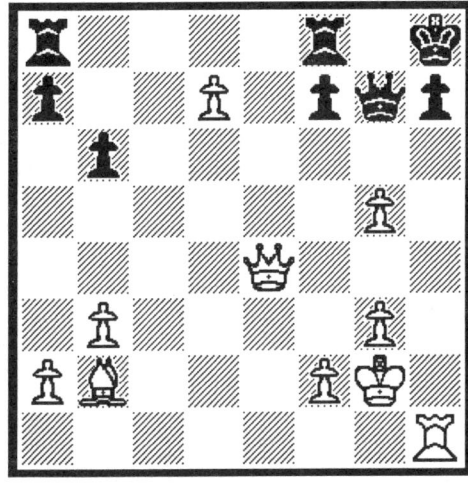

a. Write an **X** on each square to which the white Queen can move, and circle any piece the white Queen can capture.

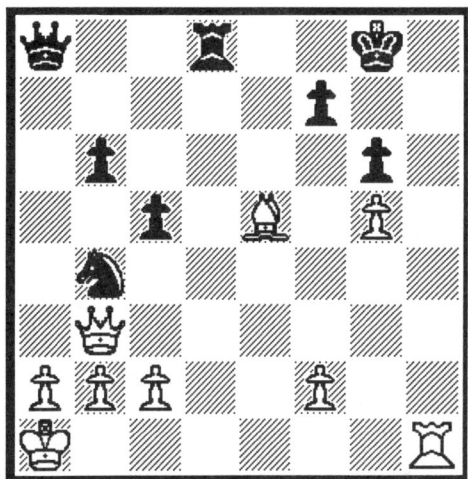

b. Write an **X** on each square to which the black Queen can move, and circle any piece the black Queen can capture.

c. Write an **X** on each square to which the black Rook can move, and circle any piece the black Rook can capture.

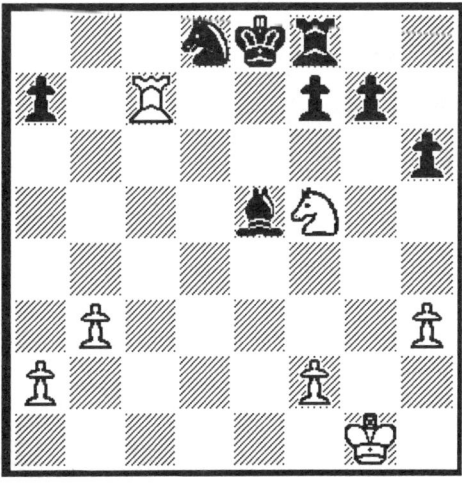

d. Write an **X** on each square to which the white Rook can move, and circle any piece the white Rook can capture.

How Bishops Move and Capture

Instruction

A Bishop can move as far as it wants along a diagonal. It must stop, however, on the square before another piece–unless the Bishop plans to capture an opponent's piece. The Bishop captures by moving onto a square occupied by the opponent's piece and then removing the piece from the board. *Remember, Bishops must stay on squares of the same color throughout a whole game.*

 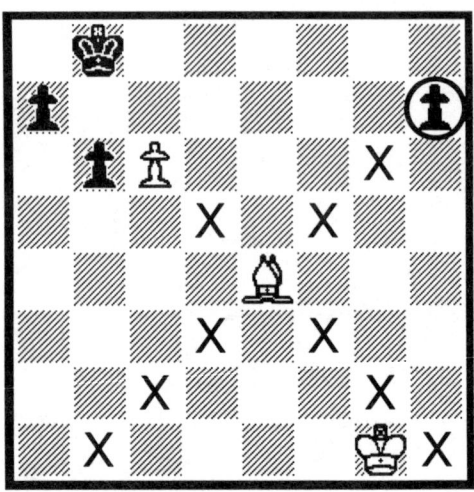

The white Bishop can move to any square marked with an **X**. This Bishop stays on black squares throughout the whole game.

The white Bishop can move to any square marked with an **X**, or capture the black pawn (circled). This Bishop stays on white squares throughout the whole game.

Activity 11

⇨ Use the diagram at right to do the following:

a. Write an **X** on each square to which the white Bishop can move.

b. Circle the piece that the white Bishop can capture.

c. On what color squares (*white* or *black*) must the white Bishop stay throughout the game?

_____
(*white* or *black*?)

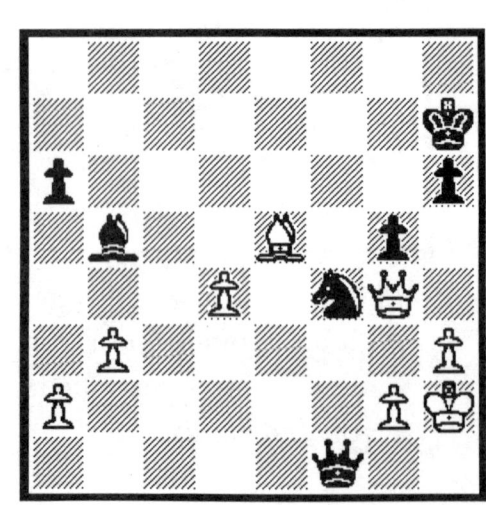

16

How Knights Move and Capture

> **Instruction**

A Knight moves two squares along a rank or file, and then one square left or right. The Knight always lands on a different color square than the square from which it begins its move. The Knight is the only piece that can jump over other pieces–either its own or the opponent's.

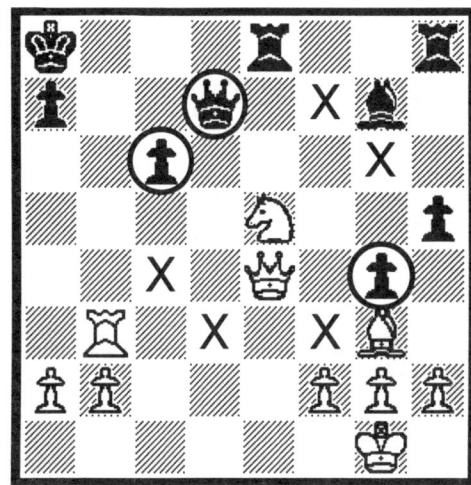

The black Knight can move to any square marked with an **X**. Arrows show how two of those moves are made.

The white Knight can move to any square marked with an **X**, or capture any of the circled pieces.

> **Activity 12**

⇨ Use the diagram at right to do the following:

a. Write an **X** on each square to which the white Knight can move.

b. Circle the pieces that the white Knight can capture.

c. Suppose the white Knight makes three moves from its present position. On what color square will it land?

_____
(*white* or *black*?)

17

Practicing Bishop and Knight Moves

Activity 13

⇨ Follow the instructions for each diagram below.

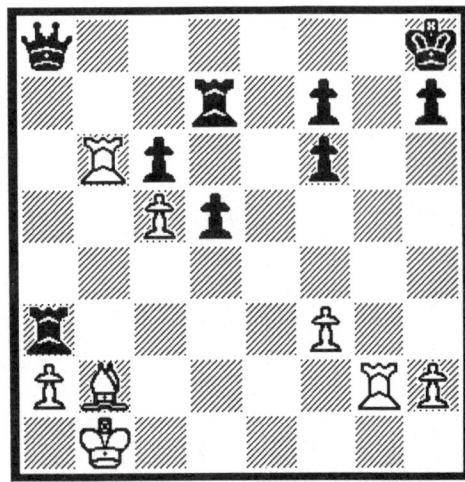

a. Write an **X** on each square to which the white Bishop can move, and circle any piece the white Bishop can capture.

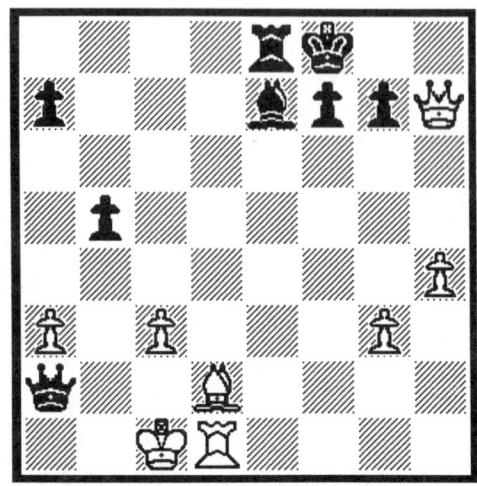

b. Write an **X** on each square to which the black Bishop can move, and circle any piece the black Bishop can capture.

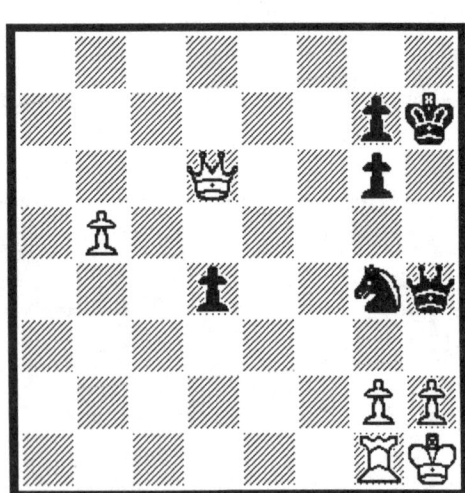

c. Write an **X** on each square to which the black Knight can move, and circle any piece the black Knight can capture.

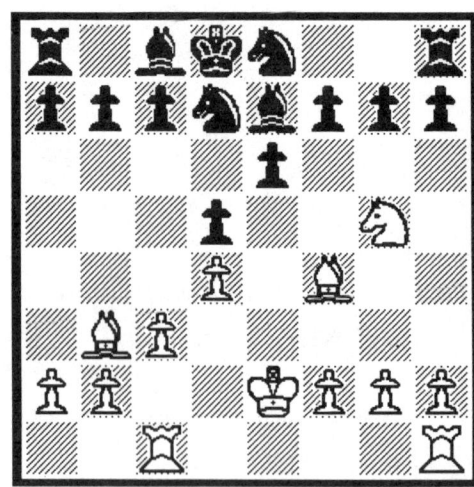

d. Write an **X** on each square to which the white Knight can move, and circle any piece the white Knight can capture.

How Pawns Move and Capture

Instruction

A pawn moves in the forward direction only, unless it captures a piece. A pawn that is in its starting position can move either one or two squares. After its first move, a pawn can move only one square at a time. A pawn capture is always a one-square move.

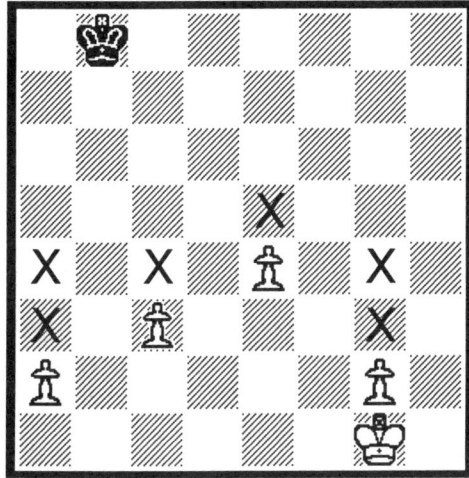

The white pawns can move to the squares marked with an **X**. Notice that pawns in their starting positions can move *either* one square or two squares.

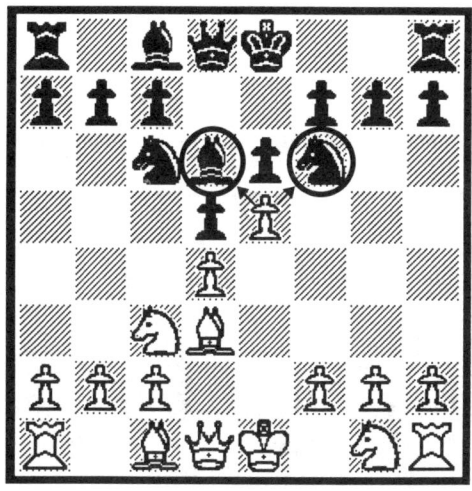

The white pawn can capture either of the circled black pieces. The pawn captures diagonally, moving one square forward to the left or right. Notice that when a pawn captures, it moves from one file to the next.

Activity 14

⇨ Use the diagram at right to do the following:

    a. Write an **X** on each square to which a white pawn can move.

    b. Circle any piece that a white pawn can capture.

    c. Draw a square around the only white pawn that can move two squares on its next move.

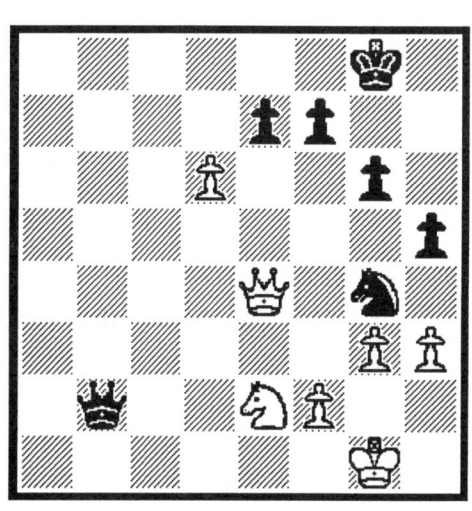

En Passant

Instruction

En passant (French for "in passing") is a special type of pawn capture involving only pawns. Your pawn may capture an opponent's pawn *en passant* when:
- your pawn is sitting on its own fifth rank, and
- your pawn is passed by the opponent's pawn on a file next to it, and
- the opponent's pawn *just moved* two squares.

Your capturing pawn is placed on the sixth rank on the square directly behind the opponent's pawn. The captured pawn is removed from the board.

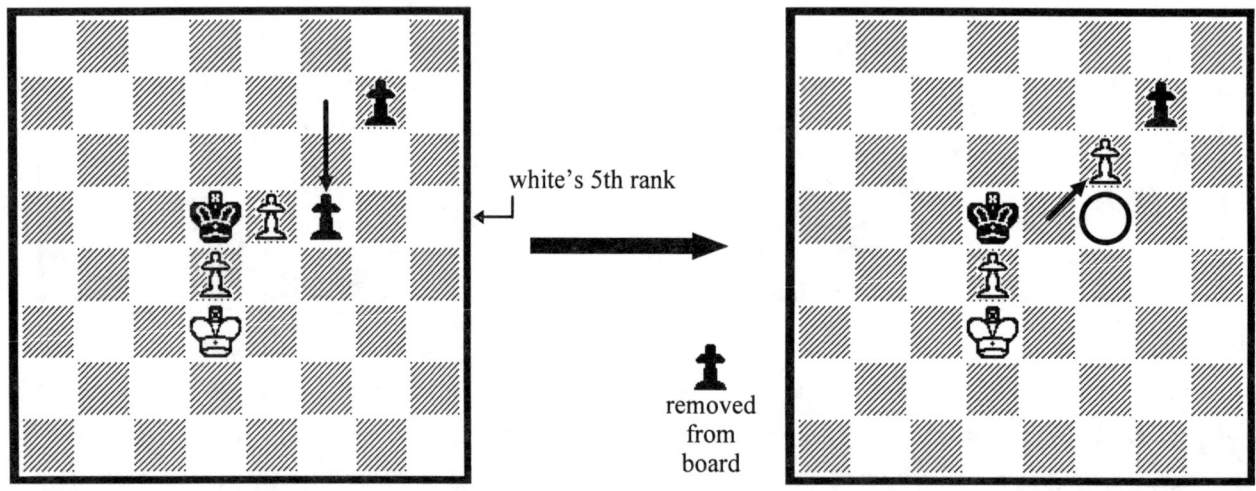

White's forward pawn is sitting on White's fifth rank. The black pawn just moved forward two squares (arrow). It is now White's move.

The white pawn captures *en passant*. The white pawn moves to the sixth rank (arrow). The black pawn is removed from the circled square.

Activity 15

⇨ On the diagram at right, Black just made the pawn move indicated by the arrow. It is now White's move.

a. Draw an arrow to the square where the white pawn moves in order to capture *en passant*.

b. Circle the black pawn that the white pawn may capture.

Promoting a Pawn

Instruction

When a pawn reaches the eighth rank (the far side of the board), it becomes a Queen, Rook, Bishop, or Knight. This is called **promoting a pawn**. *Promoting a pawn* is one of the most powerful moves in chess. The player who promotes a pawn decides which type of piece the pawn becomes. (A player can have more than one Queen at a time!)

As indicated by the arrow, White is to about to advance the pawn to the "promotion square."

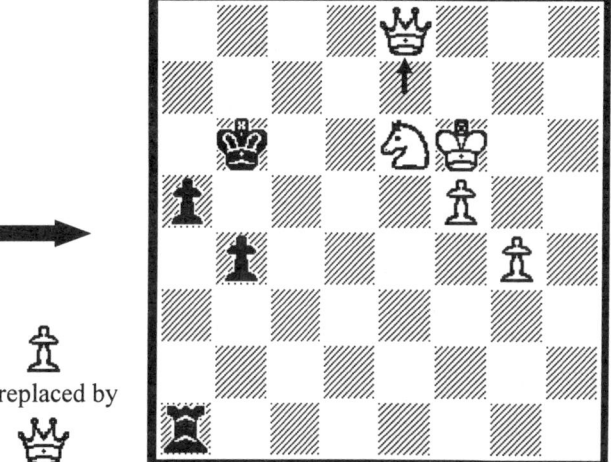

White chooses to promote the pawn to a Queen, the most powerful piece on the board.

Activity 16

➪ **a.** When a pawn is promoted to the eighth rank, what type of piece may it become?

_____   _____   _____   _____

b. On the diagram at right, circle the white pawn that can be promoted to a Queen on its next move. *Remember, on a chess diagram, the white pawns move from the bottom to the top; black pawns move from top to bottom.*

c. On the diagram at right, circle the black pawn that can be promoted to a Queen on its next move.

Practicing Pawn Moves

Activity 17

⇨ Follow the instructions for each diagram below.

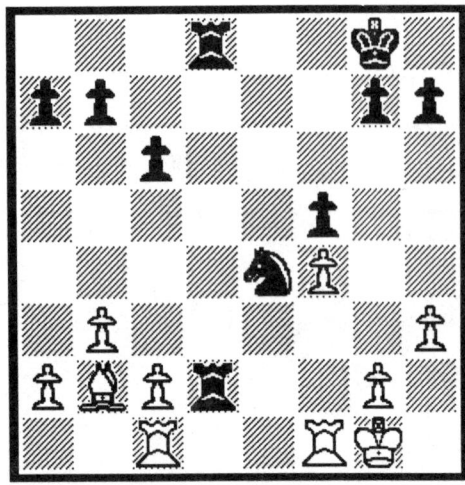

a. Circle each pawn that can move two squares on its next move.

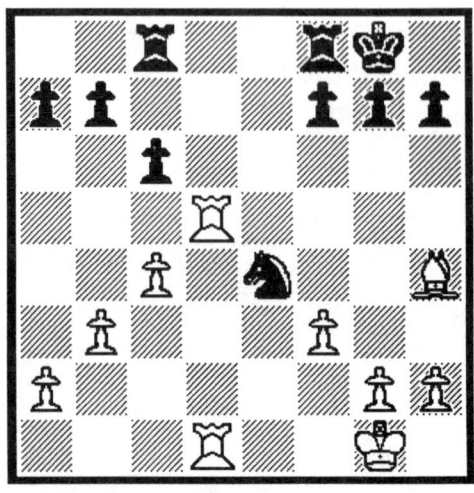

b. Circle each pawn that can capture an opponent's piece on its next move. Draw a square around each threatened piece.

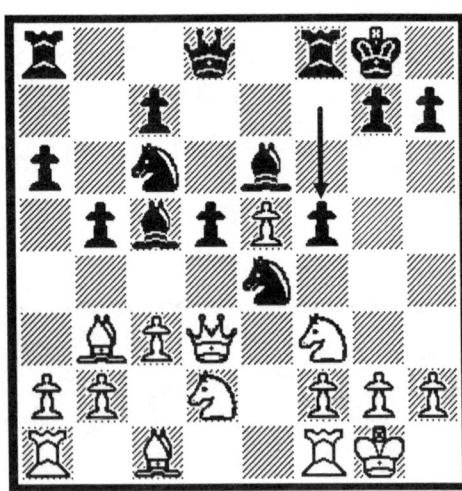

c. Black just made the pawn move indicated by the arrow. Draw an arrow to the square where a white pawn can move to make an *en passant* capture. Circle the black pawn that will be captured.

d. Circle each pawn that can be promoted to a Queen on its next move.

Checking the King

> **Instruction**

Check is a move that directly attacks the opponent's King. Any chess piece, except the King, can check the opponent's King. If in check, a King must immediately get out of check. A King can get out of check in three ways:
- Move out of check.
- Block the check with another piece.
- Capture the checking piece.

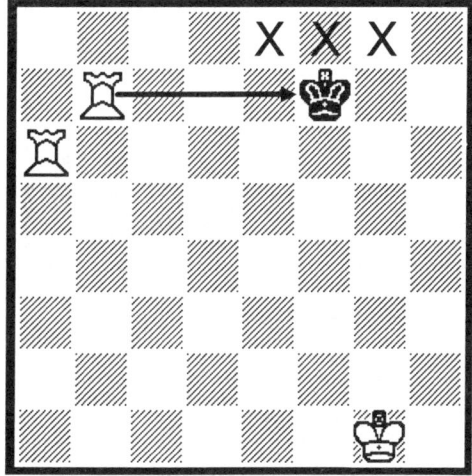

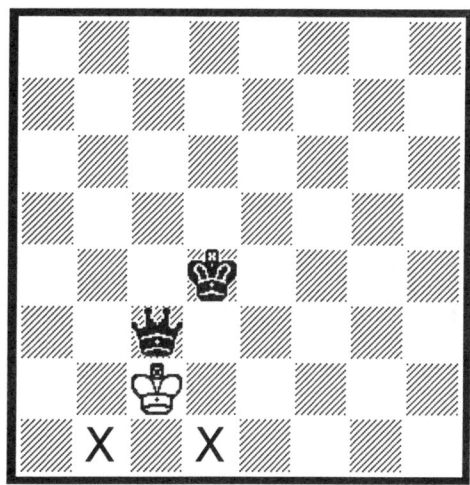

The black King is in check by the white Rook (arrow). The black King can move out of check by moving to any of the three squares marked with an **X**. These safe squares are called "flight squares."

The white King is in check by the black Queen. The white King has two flight squares, each marked with an **X**. The game would be over if the King could not get out of check!

> **Activity 18**

⇨ Use the diagram at right to do the following:

a. Circle the white piece that is checking the black King.

b. Write an **X** on the flight square to which the black King can move.

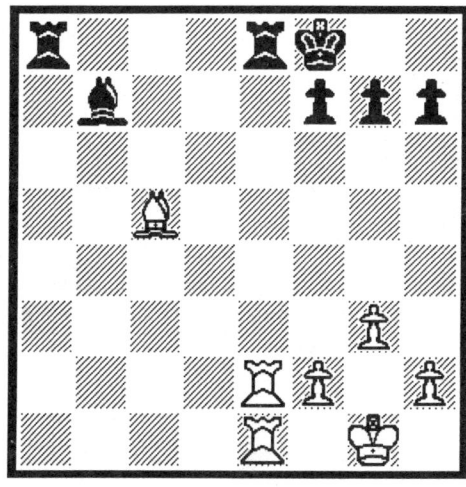

Practicing Checking

Activity 19

⇨ Draw an arrow on each diagram below to show the checking move.

a. Black to move the Queen and check the white King.

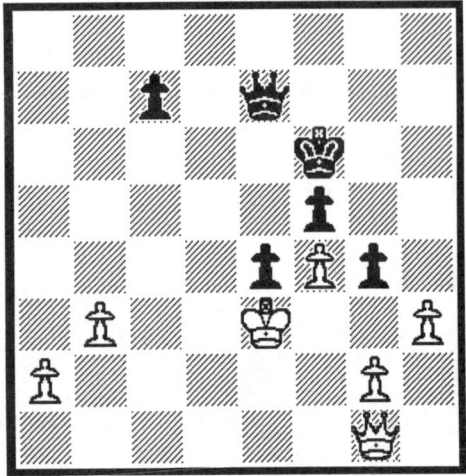

Black to move.

b. White to move the Rook and check the black King.

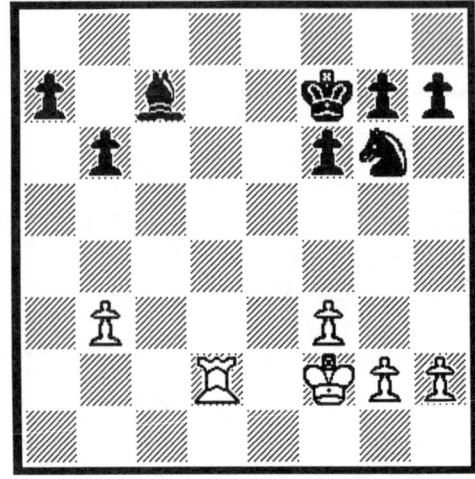

White to move.

c. White to move the Bishop and check the black King.

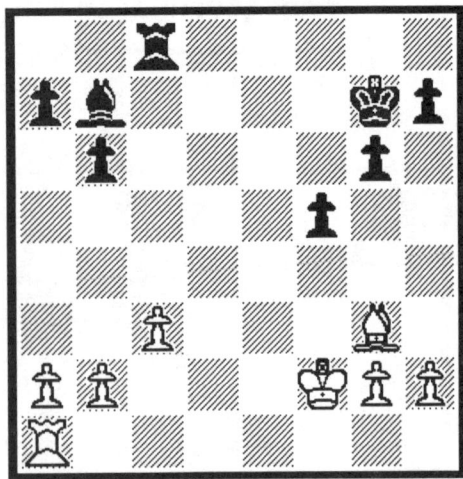

White to move.

d. Black to move the Knight and check the white King.

Black to move.

Two Moves a King <u>Cannot</u> Make

> Instruction

A King cannot move onto a square on which:
- the King would remain in check; or
- the King would move into check.

In the diagram at right, the black King is in check by the white Rook (arrow). The black King must move out of check. However, the black King cannot:
- move to either square marked with an **X**, because the King would remain in check by the white Rook; or
- move to the square marked with a circle, because the King would be moving onto a square guarded by the white Knight. Moving to this square would be moving into check.

The black King's only move is to the square indicated by the arrow.

> Activity 20

⇨ In each diagram below, explain why the white King cannot move to the circled square: *cannot remain in check* or *cannot move into check*.

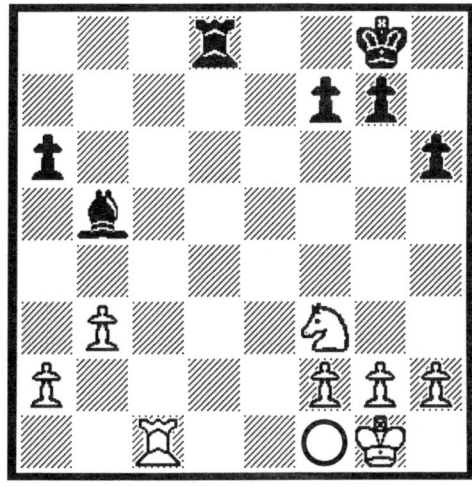

a. _____

b. _____

_____

_____

Two More Moves a King **Cannot** Make

| Instruction |

A King also cannot:
- capture an opponent's piece that is guarded by another piece, or
- move onto a square that is next to the opponent's King.

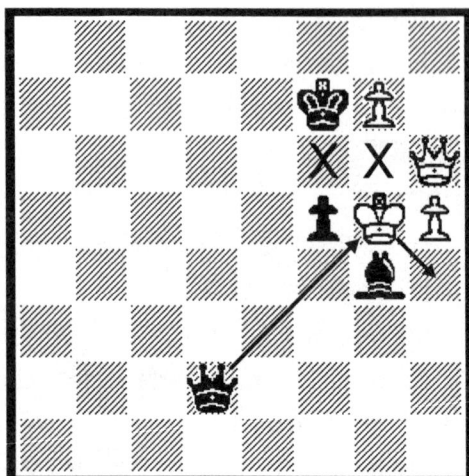

In the diagram at right, the white King is in check by the black Queen (arrow). The white King must move out of check. However, the white King cannot:
- move to either square marked with an **X**, because the King would be moving onto a square that is next to the black King; or
- take the black Bishop, because the Bishop is guarded by a black pawn; or
- take the black pawn, because the pawn is guarded by the black Bishop.

The white King's only move is to the square indicated by the arrow.

| Activity 21 |

⇨ In each diagram, explain why the black King cannot move to the circled square: *cannot capture a guarded piece* or *cannot move next to the opponent's King*.

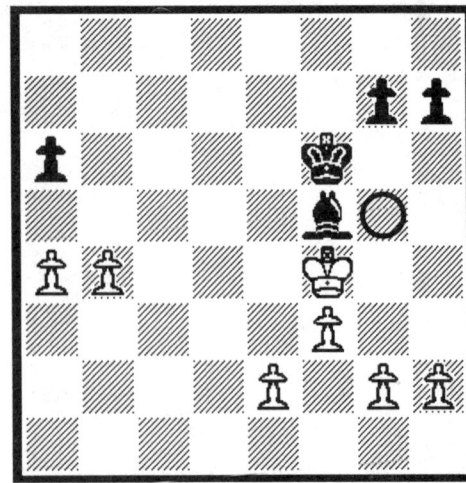

a. _____

b. _____

Getting Out of Check

> **Instruction**

When a player's King is in check, the player <u>must</u> get the King out of check. The player can do any one of the following that is possible:
- **Flee:** Move the King to a safe flight square. *A safe flight square is a square that is neither guarded by an opponent's piece nor next to the opponent's King.*
- **Interpose:** Move a piece between the King and the checking piece.
- **Capture:** Take the checking piece.

> **Activity 22**

⇨ **a.** Under each diagram, circle how Black can get out of check: *flee*, *interpose* or *capture*.

b. Draw an arrow on each diagram to show the move that gets the black King out of check. Circle any captured piece.

Flee?   Interpose?   Capture?

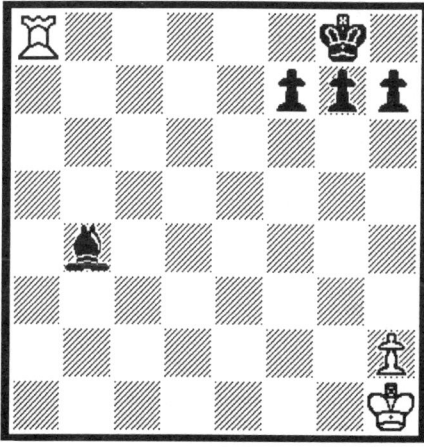

Flee?   Interpose?   Capture?

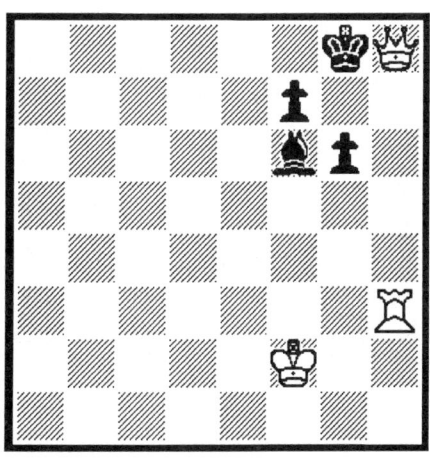

Flee?   Interpose?   Capture?

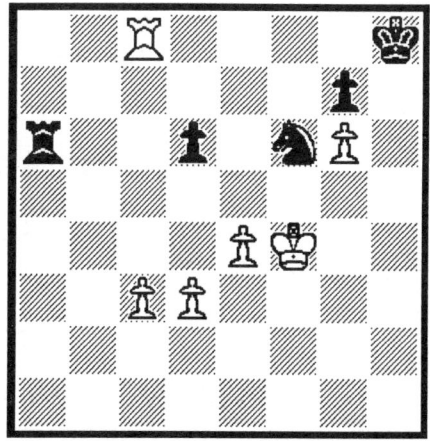

Flee?   Interpose?   Capture?

Castling

> **Instruction**

Castling is a single move that involves both the King and one Rook. To castle, the King moves <u>two</u> <u>squares</u> toward the Rook it will castle with. Then, that Rook moves to the other side of the King. Castling is a move that protects the King from attack.

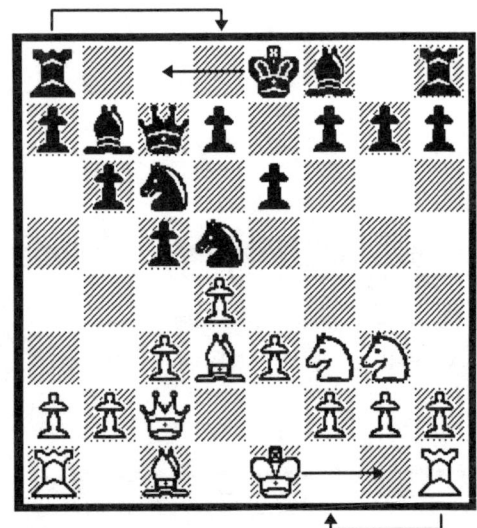

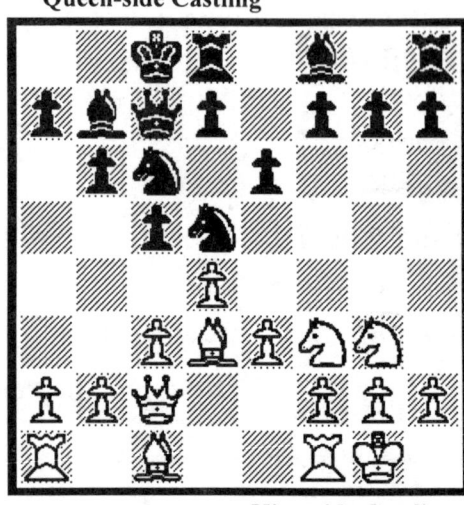

Both black and white pieces can castle. Black has prepared to castle *Queen-side*. White has prepared to castle *King-side*.

Black has castled Queen-side. White has castled King-side. *During a game, each King can castle only once.*

> **Activity 23**

➡ Use the diagram at the right to complete the following:

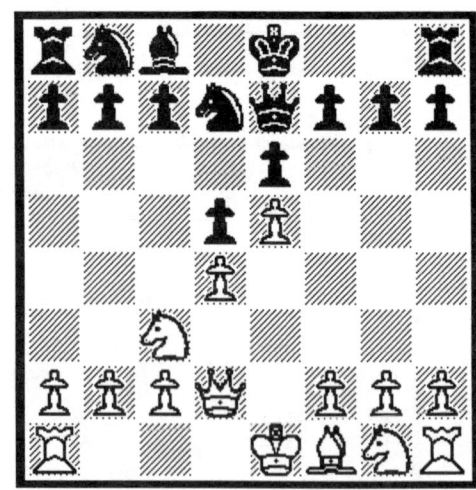

a. Black can castle _____.
   (*King-side* or *Queen-side?*)

b. White can castle _____.
   (*King-side* or *Queen-side?*)

c. Write a **K** on the square where each King lands after castling, and an **R** where each Rook lands.

d. During a game, how many times can each King castle? _____
   number

When Can A King Castle?

Instruction

A King can castle when:
- The King is on its original square and has not yet moved.
- The castling Rook is on its original square and has not yet moved.
- The squares between the King and castling Rook are empty.

A King cannot castle when:
- The King is in check.
- The King would pass through check or land in check while castling.
- The King or castling Rook has already moved.
- Any square between the King and castling Rook is occupied by a piece.

Activity 24

⇨ Answer the two questions beside each diagram below.

a. Why can't Black castle King-side on the next move?

b. Why can't White castle at all this game?

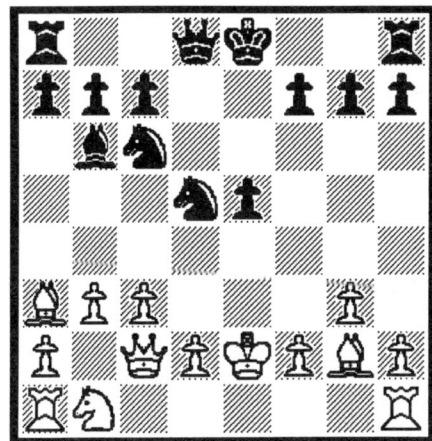

c. Why can't White castle on the next move?

d. Why can't Black castle King-side on the next move?

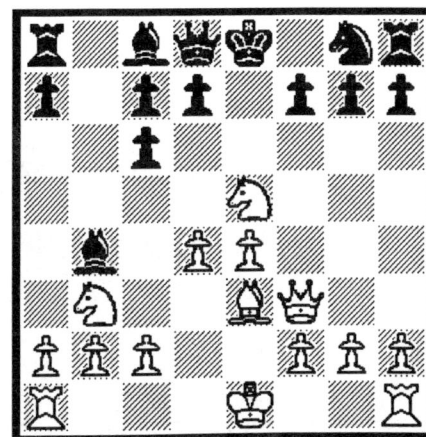

29

Checkmate

| Instruction |

Checkmate is a position in which one King is in check and cannot get out of check. A checkmate ends a chess game. For example, if the white King gets *checkmated*, the player with the black pieces wins the game. The checkmated King is unable to *capture* the checking piece, *interpose* to block the check, or *flee* to a safe flight square.

Checkmate!

The black King is checkmated by the white Rook. The black King cannot capture the Rook, has no piece to interpose, and has no safe flight square. White wins this game.

Checkmate!

The white King is checkmated by the black Queen. The white King cannot capture the black Queen because the Queen is protected by the black King. The white King has no safe flight square. Black wins this game.

| Activity 25 |

➪ Use the diagram at right to do the following:

a. Circle the white piece that is checkmating the black King.

b. Name the checkmating piece: _____

c. Why can't the black King capture the Queen?

_____

_____

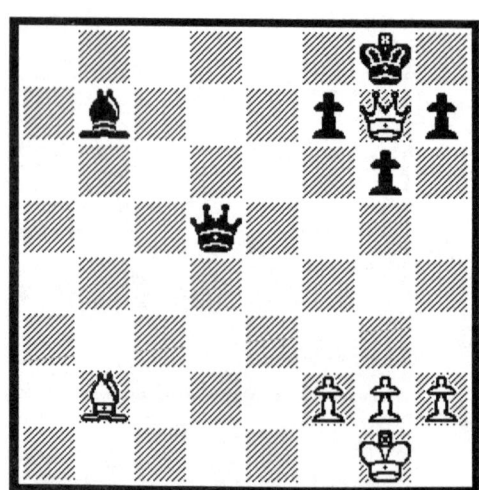

Practicing Queen Checkmates

Activity 26

⇨ Draw an arrow on each diagram below to show the checkmating Queen move. Circle any captured piece that results in checkmate.

a. White to move the Queen and checkmate in one move.

White to move.

b. Black to move the Queen and checkmate in one move.

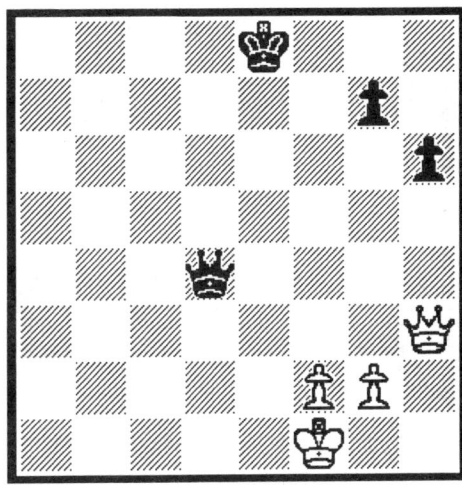

Black to move.

c. White to move the Queen and checkmate in one move.

White to move.

d. Black to move the Queen and checkmate in one move.

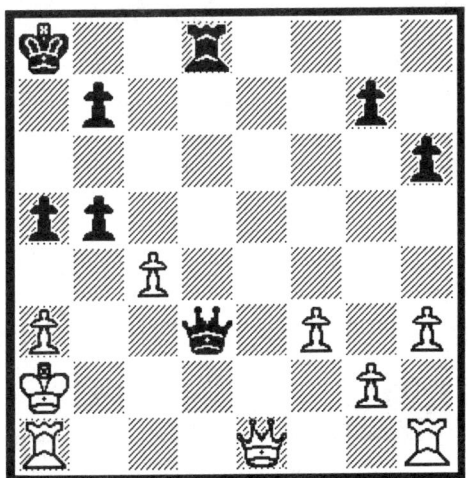

Black to move.

31

Practicing Rook Checkmates

Activity 27

⇨ Draw an arrow on each diagram below to show the checkmating Rook move.

a. Black to move the Rook and checkmate in one move.

Black to move.

b. White to move the Rook and checkmate in one move.

White to move.

c. Black to move a Rook and checkmate in one move.

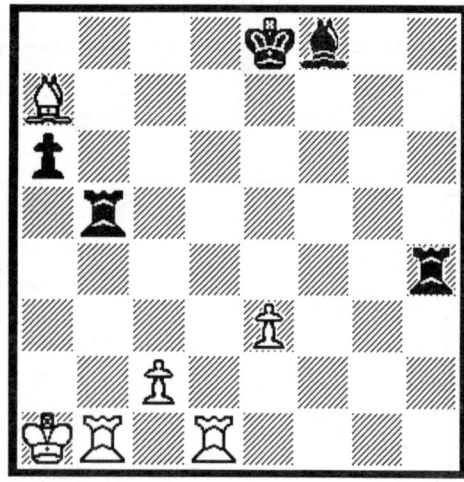

Black to move.

d. White to move the Rook and checkmate in one move.

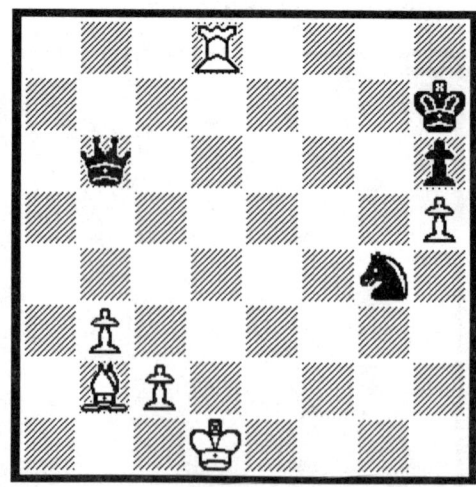

White to move.

Practicing Bishop, Knight, and Pawn Checkmates

Activity 28

➪ Draw an arrow on each diagram below to show the checkmating move.

a. White to move the Bishop and checkmate in one move.

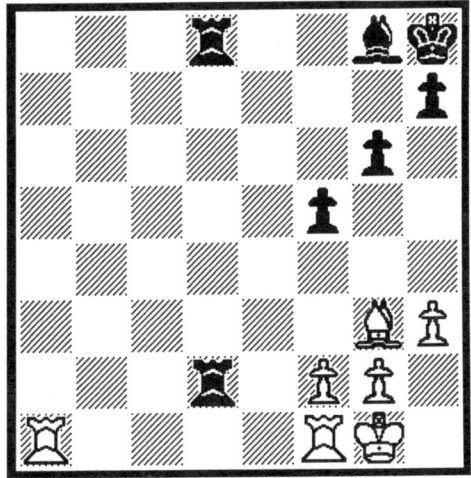

White to move.

b. Black to move the Knight and checkmate in one move.

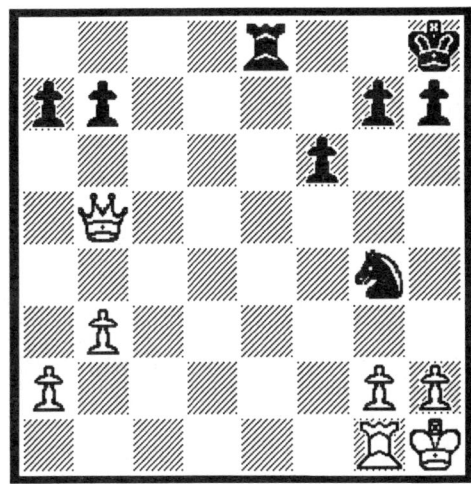

Black to move.

c. White to move the Bishop and checkmate in one move.

White to move.

d. Black to move a pawn and checkmate in one move.

Black to move.

Stalemate Draw

Instruction

A chess game is **drawn** when neither player wins. One type of **draw** that ends many of the games played by beginners is called a **stalemate draw**. In a stalemate draw, one player *stalemates* (quite often accidentally) the other player's King.

A King is *stalemated* when that King:
- cannot legally move, and
- is not in check, and
- none of its pieces can move.

A Stalemate Draw

In the diagram at right, the black King just moved forward (arrow). The white King is not in check, but it cannot now legally move. The only other white piece, the white pawn, is blocked by the black pawn. Neither of the white pieces can move. This game is a stalemate; it is a draw. Although Black is ahead in **material** (value of pieces), Black does not win this game.

Activity 29

⇨ The two games below are over. Under each diagram, circle how the game ended: *stalemate draw* or *checkmate*.

Stalemate Draw?   Checkmate?

Stalemate Draw?   Checkmate?

Other Types of Draws

> **Instruction**

In addition to a stalemate draw, there are five other ways in which a chess game can end in a draw.

Lack of Checkmating Material. A chess game is drawn when each player has a lack of checkmating material. Here are four of the most common lack-of-material draws:
- A lone King against a lone King.
- A King and Bishop against a lone King.
- A King and Knight against a lone King.
- A King and two Knights against a lone King.

Perpetual Check. A chess game is drawn when one player can endlessly check the opponent's King. The checked King cannot escape the series of checks.

Three Move Repetition. A chess game is drawn when a player correctly claims that the same position is about to be repeated for the third time, then makes the move. The three repetitions may occur right after one another, or they may be separated by many moves.

Fifty Move Rule. A chess game is drawn when a player correctly claims that 50 moves have been made by each player without either player capturing a piece or moving a pawn.

Agreement. A chess game is drawn when both players agree to a draw.

> **Activity 30**

⇨ **a.** In the diagram at right, the game ended in a draw. Explain why.

_____

_____

_____

b. Name the type of draw that occurs when one player puts the other player's King in an endless series of checks.

_____

Choosing to Underpromote a Pawn

Instruction

In some positions, a player should **underpromote** a pawn–promote it to a piece *other than a Queen*. In the diagram at right, it is White's move. White chooses to promote the pawn (arrow). White can promote the pawn to a Queen, but the game would end as a stalemate draw. Black would not have a legal move. By choosing to promote the pawn to a Rook, however, White avoids the stalemate draw and goes on to win easily.

Activity 31

a. In the diagram at right, what will be the result of the game if it is White's move and White promotes the pawn to a Queen?

_____

_____

_____

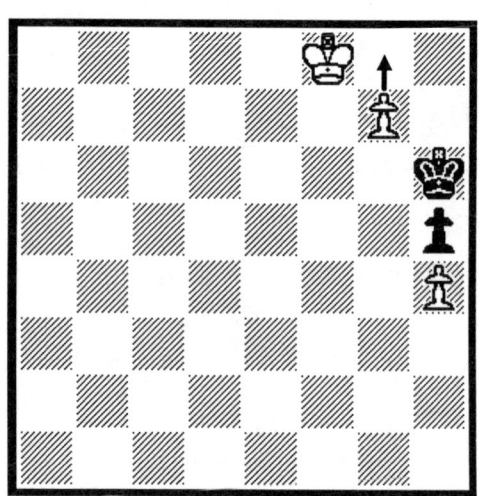

b. In the diagram at right, should Black promote the pawn to a Queen, Rook, Bishop, or Knight? Give a reason for your answer.

_____

_____

_____

Piece Value

Instruction

According to the rules of chess, a chess game can end in one of three ways:
- One player checkmates the other.
- One player resigns.
- The game is drawn.

Nothing in the rules talks about the *value* of pieces. However, chess players know that, in general, pieces are not equal. A Queen, for example, is by far the most powerful piece on the board in almost all positions.

As a guide for beginners, each piece, except the King, is said to have a numerical value. The King is not given point value because it is never captured or traded for other pieces. Knowing point values helps a beginner decide if trading one piece for another is a good idea. As players become more skilled in chess, the idea of piece value naturally will become a more subtle concept. Below is a list of approximate piece values.

King	No value assigned
Queen	9 points
Rook	5 points
Bishop	3 points
Knight	3 points
Pawn	1 point

Activity 32

➪ Match each combination of pieces on the left with the combination of pieces on the right that has the same point value.

_____ 1. ♝♞   a) ♕

_____ 2. ♞   b) ♗♙♙

_____ 3. ♜♝♟   c) ♖♖

_____ 4. ♜   d) ♖♙

_____ 5. ♛♟   e) ♙♙♙

Checkmate Challenge I

Activity 33

The activity below will challenge your ability to find a checkmating move. Your goal is to find the correct move in each diagram. You decide which piece to move and where to move it! Good luck!

⇨ Draw an arrow on each diagram below to show the checkmating move.

a. White to move and checkmate in one move.

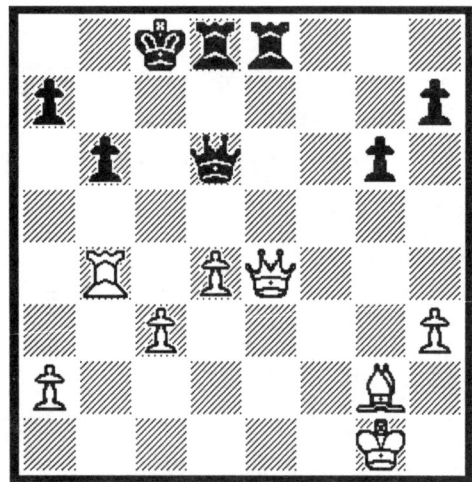

White to move.

b. Black to move and checkmate in one move.

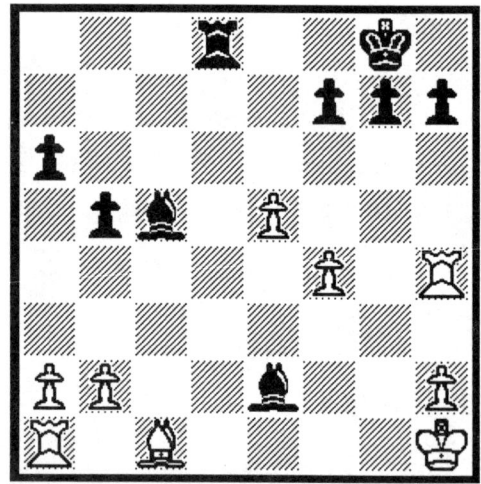

Black to move.

c. White to move and checkmate in one move.

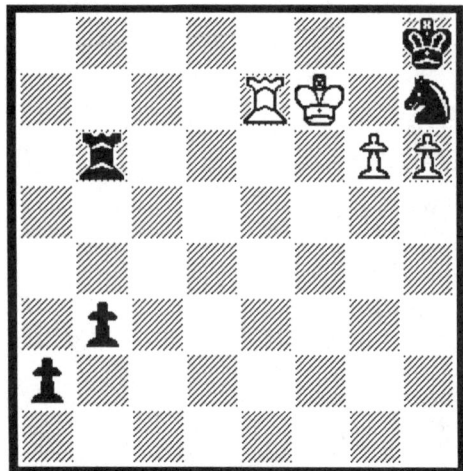

White to move.

d. Black to move and checkmate in one move.

Black to move.

Checkmate Challenge II

Activity 34

In this activity, you are to find a move that *prevents checkmate*! For example, in diagram **a**, you find a move for Black that prevents White from checkmating on the next move. [Hint: As a first step, find the opponent's checkmating move!]

⇨ Draw an arrow on each diagram to show a move that protects against checkmate.

a. Black to move and prevent White from checkmating.

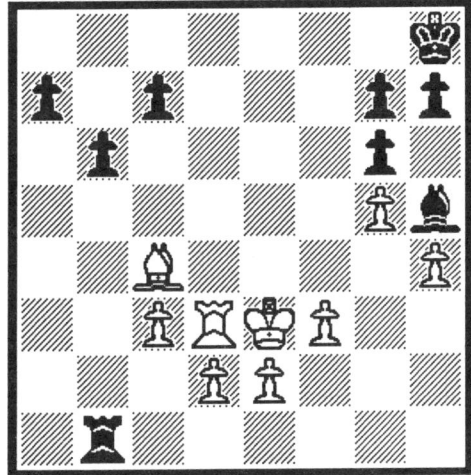

Black to move.

b. White to move and prevent Black from checkmating.

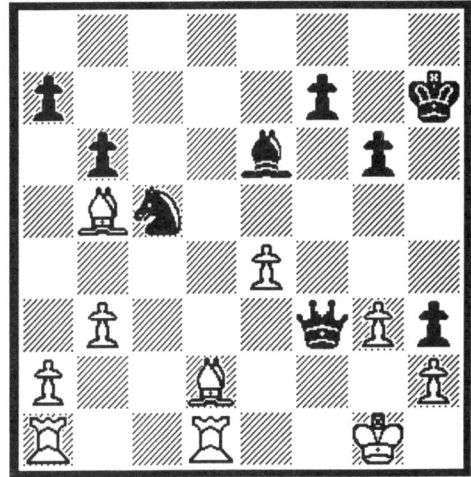

White to move.

c. Black to move and prevent White from checkmating.

Black to move.

d. White to move and prevent Black from checkmating.

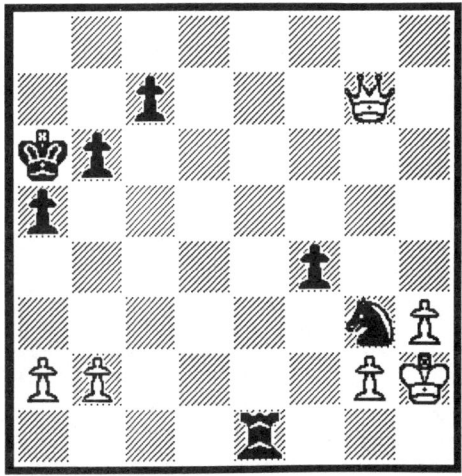

White to move.

39

Learning Algebraic Notation

Instruction

The next step after learning to play is learning how to **record a chess game**—keeping a written list of moves. To enable you to do this, each square on a chess board is given a name. *A square is named as a file letter followed by a rank number.* This method of naming squares is called **algebraic notation**.

- Files are lettered from a to h, using lower-case letters.
- Ranks are numbered from 1 to 8.

Algebraic Notation

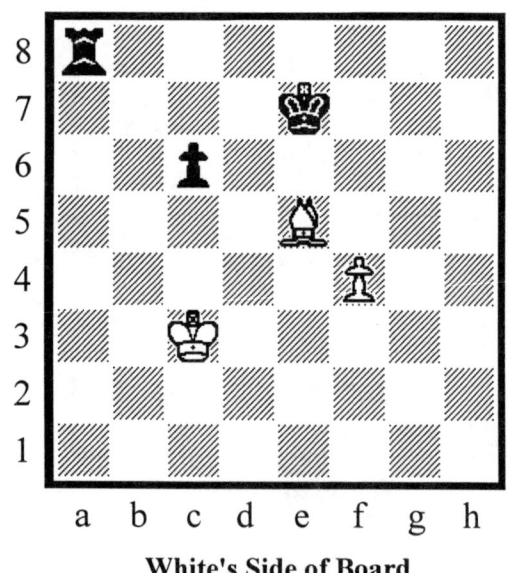

White's Side of Board

Examples:

- The white King is on **c3**.   [c file, 3rd rank]
- The black King is on **e7**.   [e file, 7th rank]
- The white pawn is on **f4**.   [f file, 4th rank]
- The black pawn is on **c6**.   [c file, 6th rank]
- The white Bishop is on **e5**.   [e file, 5th rank]
- The black Rook is on **a8**.   [a file, 8th rank]

Activity 35

⇨ Using the board at right, write the name of the square on which each piece is sitting.

black King: _____

white King: _____

black pawn: _____

white pawn: _____

black Queen: _____

white Rook: _____

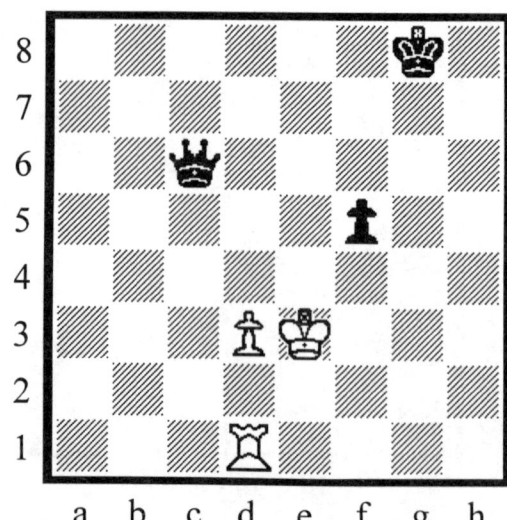

Recording Chess Moves

Instruction

To **record a chess move**, you do two things:
- Identify the piece being moved. Except for a Knight and a pawn, write the first letter of the name of the piece. Use capital letters to identify pieces (**K**, **Q**, **R**, **B**, and **N**). Write **K** to identify the King and **N** to identify the Knight.
- Write the name of the square *to which the piece is moved*. To identify a pawn move, you write only the name of the square to which the pawn is moved.

Letter Symbols for Chess Pieces

K = King	**B** = Bishop	**R** = Rook
Q = Queen	**N** = Knight	nothing = Pawn

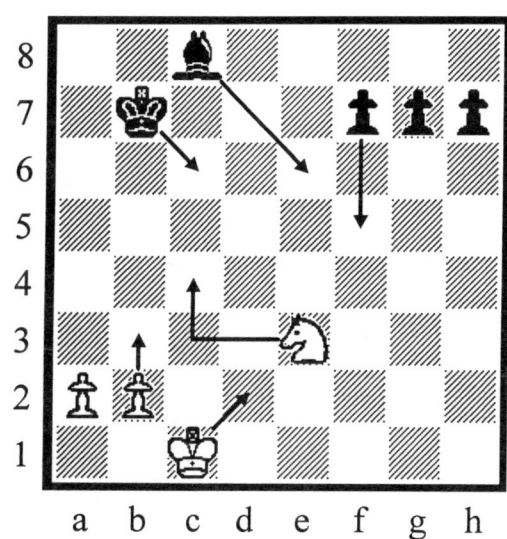

Example moves are indicated by arrows on the diagram at left.
- The white pawn's move is written **b3**.
- The black pawn's move is written **f5**.
- The white Knight's move is written **Nc4**.
- The black Bishop's move is written **Be6**.
- The white King's move is written **Kd2**.
- The black King's move is written **Kc6**.

Activity 36

⇨ On the board at right, piece moves are shown by arrows. Record each move in algebraic notation.

white pawn: _____   black pawn: _____

white Knight: _____   black Bishop: _____

white Queen: _____   black Rook: _____

white King: _____   black Queen: _____

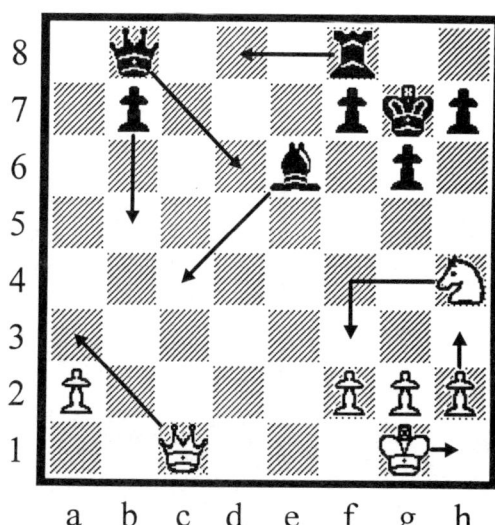

41

Capturing, Castling, Checking and Checkmating

> **Instruction**

Special symbols are used to show capturing, castling, checking and checkmating.
- When capturing, write the name of the square on which the capture takes place.
  You do not need to name the captured piece.

Symbol	Definition	Example	Meaning
×	captures	N×d4	Knight captures the piece sitting on d4.
+	check	Qa5+	Queen moves to a5 and checks King.
#	checkmate	Rc8#	Rook moves to c8 and checkmates.
0-0	King-side castling	0-0	Player castles King-side.
0-0-0	Queen-side castling	0-0-0	Player castles Queen-side.

> **Activity 37**

➪ Write the move indicated by the arrow on each diagram. For each move, use one or more of the symbols (×, +, #, 0-0, or 0-0-0) as needed.

a.
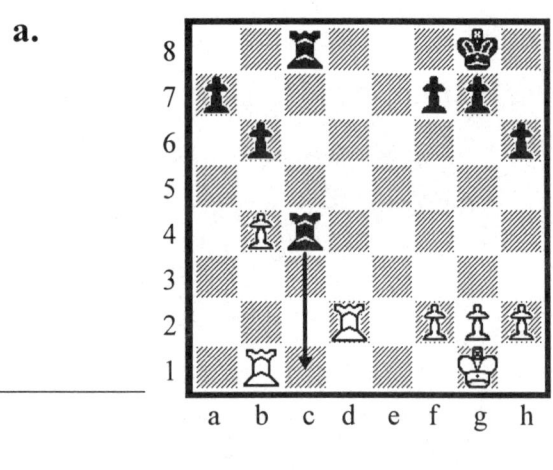

b.
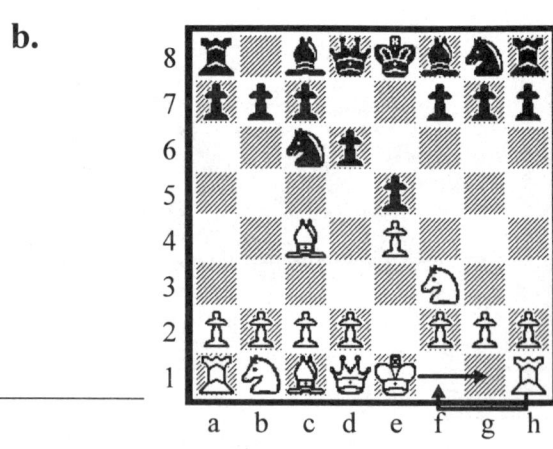

c.
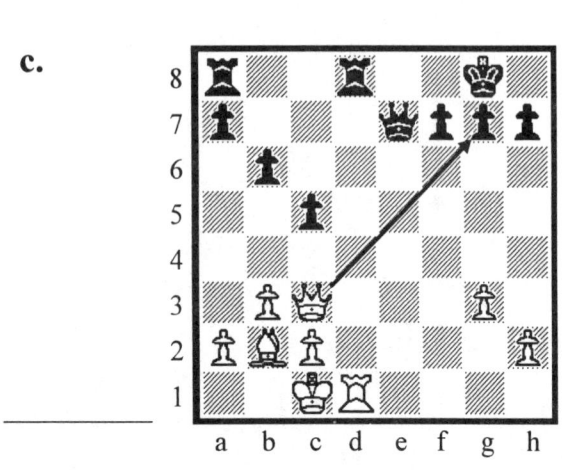

d.
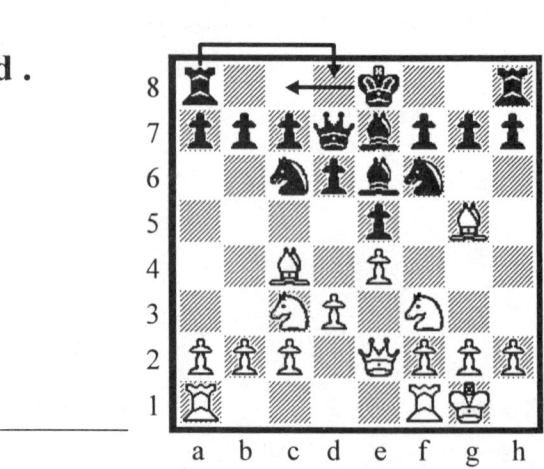

42

Avoiding Confusion With Like Pieces

Instruction

Sometimes you can move either of two *like pieces* (two knights or two rooks) to the same square. When this happens, you must identify which piece you are moving.
- To identify one of two like pieces, write the letter of the piece *and its file letter*.
- If both pieces are on the same file, write the letter of the piece *and its rank number*.

At right, Black can use either Rook to capture the white Bishop on d8.
- To capture with the a8 Rook, Black records the move as **Ra×d8**.
- To capture with the f8 Rook, Black records the move as **Rf×d8**.

White can use either Knight to capture the black pawn on c5.
- To capture with the d3 Knight, White records the move as **N3×c5**.
- To capture with the e4 Knight, White records the move as **N7×c5**.

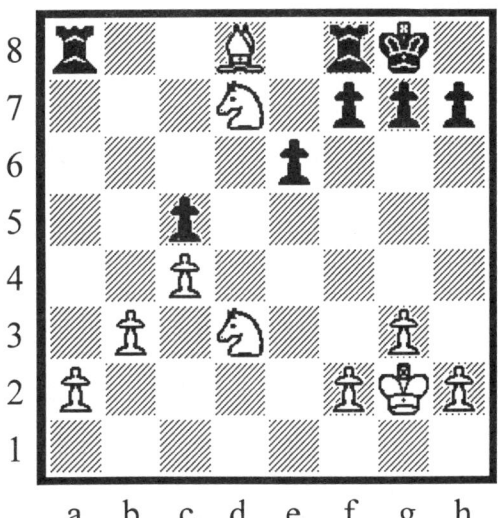

Activity 38

⇨ Looking at the board at right, how would you record the following moves?

    a. White uses the Rook on a8 _____
        to capture the black Queen.

    b. White uses the Rook on a3 _____
        to capture the black Queen.

    c. Black uses the Knight on f5 _____
        to capture the white Bishop.

    d. Black uses the Knight on g4 _____
        to capture the white Bishop.

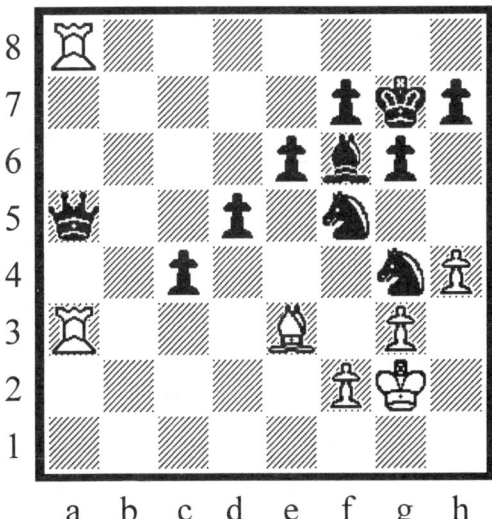

King Pawn Opening

Instruction

The first moves of a chess game (called the **opening**) are very important. Beginning players should try to accomplish three things with opening moves:
- control center squares with one or two pawns
- develop minor pieces early—knights and bishops
- castle to protect the King

The most popular (and safest!) opening for beginners is a King pawn opening. The first 8 moves of a typical King pawn opening are given below.

	White	Black
1.	e4	e5
2.	Nf3	Nc6
3.	Bc4	Nf6
4.	Nc3	Bd7
5.	O-O	O-O
6.	d4	d6
7.	a6	Bd7
8.	Bg5	h6

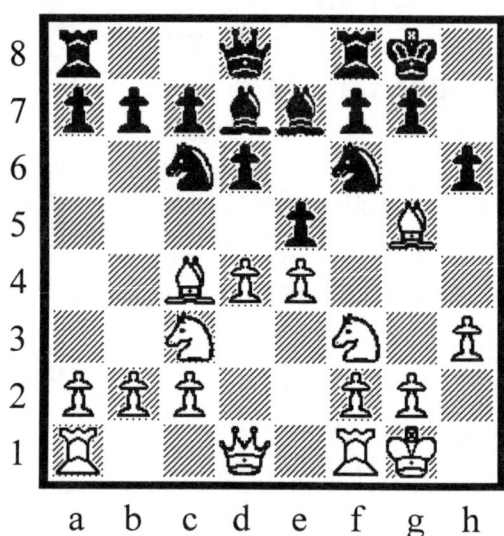

Activity 39

⇨ On the board at right, each player has made 5 moves of another King pawn opening. The first 4 moves are listed below.

Fill in the blank lines to show each player's 5th move.

	White	Black
1.	e4	e5
2.	Nf3	Nc6
3.	d3	Nf6
4.	Bg5	Be7
5.	____	____

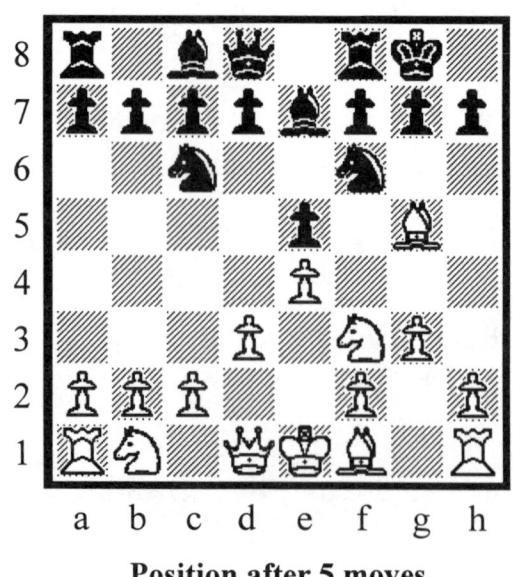

Position after 5 moves.

Queen Pawn Opening

> Instruction

A second popular opening is a Queen pawn opening. This opening also is designed to gain center control with a pawn, develop minor pieces quickly, and castle to provide the King with safety.

As with King pawn openings, Queen pawn openings have many variations. Students are encouraged to try different variations to see which they like best.

The first 8 moves of a typical Queen pawn opening are given below.

	White	Black
1.	d4	d5
2.	c4	e6
3.	Nc3	Nf6
4.	Bg5	Be7
5.	e3	0-0
6.	Nf3	Nbd7
7.	Bd3	c6
8.	0-0	h6

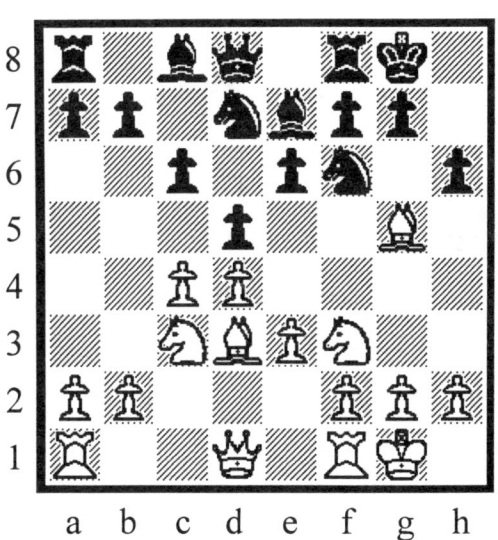

> Activity 40

⇨ On the board at right, each player has made 5 moves of another Queen pawn opening. The first 4 moves are listed below.

Fill in the blank lines to show each player's 5th move.

	White	Black
1.	d4	Nf6
2.	c4	e6
3.	Nf3	Bb4+
4.	Nc3	B×c3
5.	_____	_____

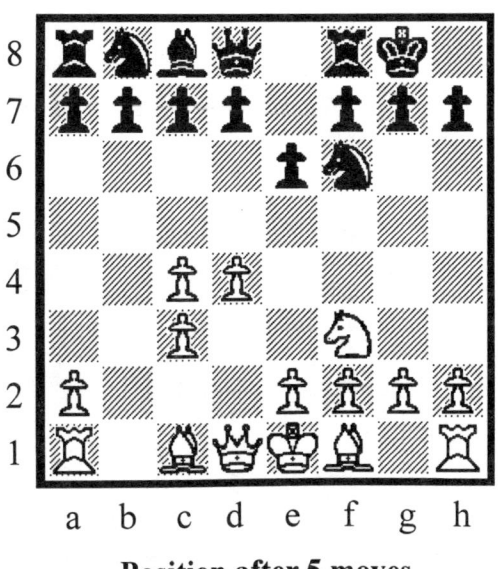

Position after 5 moves.

Special Recording Symbols

> **Instruction**

When you read games that are recorded in chess books and magazines, you may see the special symbols listed below.

Symbol	Definition
!	a good move [Example: **Q×e7!**]
?	a weak move [a move that weakens a player's game. Example: **N×b3?**]
??	a blunder [a major mistake; a game-ending mistake. Example: **Rc4??**]
e.p.	*en passant* [a pawn capture by en passant. Example: **e×d6, e.p.**]
=	equals [used to show pawn promotion. Example: **c8 = Q** means a player moves the c pawn to the 8th rank and chooses a Queen]

> **Activity 41**

⇨ Write the move indicated by the arrow on each diagram. Following the move, write the symbol (!, ?, ??, e.p., or = Q) that best describes the move.

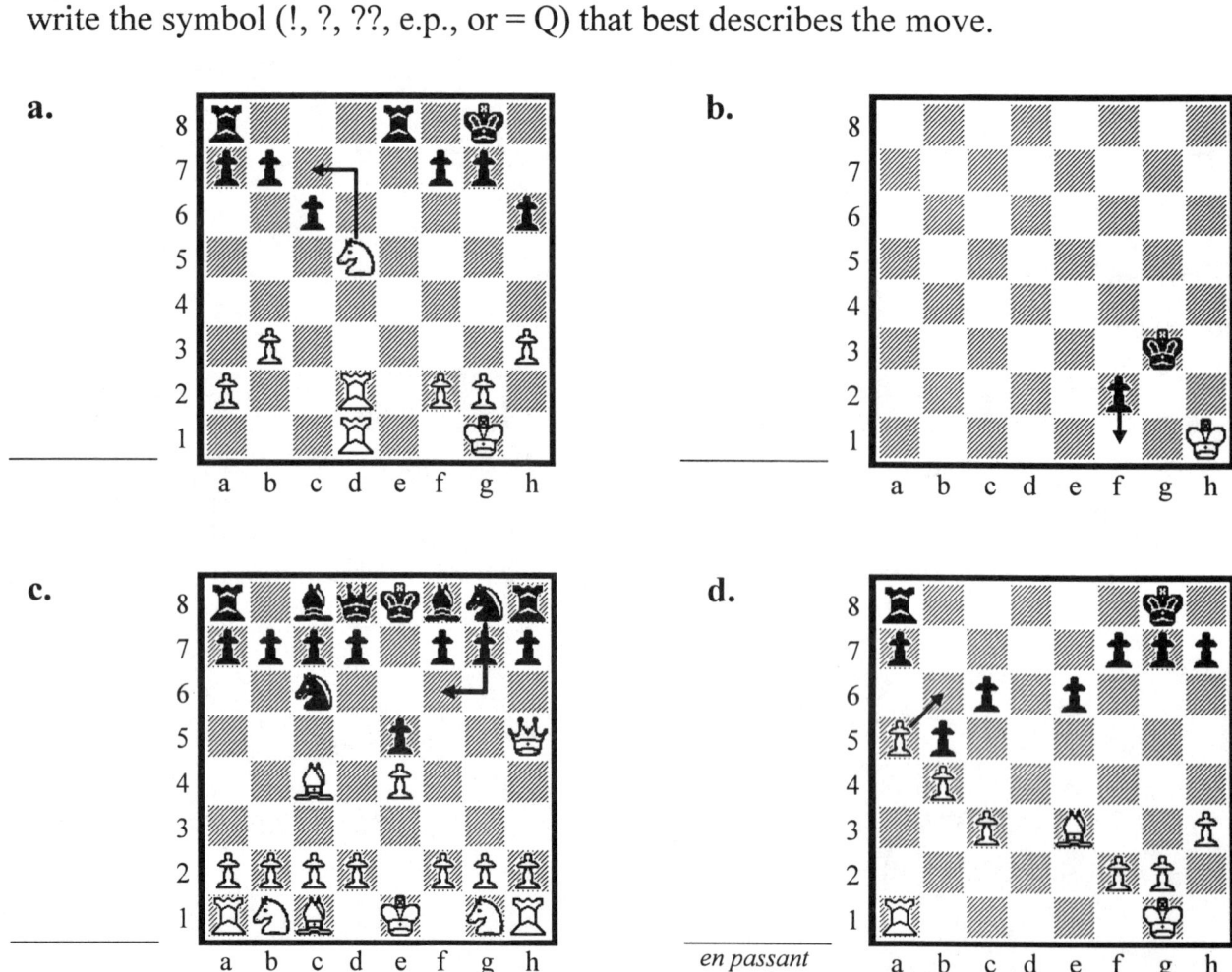

d. *en passant* capture

46

Game Rules and Courtesies

Instruction

Congratulations on becoming a chess player! As a player, you may be interested in the game rules and courtesies listed below. These are especially important in tournament play. After completing this page, use the Answer Key (starting on the next page) to check your answers to all activities. Good luck in all of your chess games.

Game Rules

1. To decide who plays white and who plays black, players can flip a coin or **draw for colors**. In a tournament, the tournament director decides.
2. In every chess game, White moves first to begin the game.
3. Players play **touch move**. If a player touches a piece, that player must move the touched piece if it is legally possible. If a player touches one of the opponent's pieces, that player must capture the opponent's piece if it is legally possible.
4. When straightening out-of-position pieces during a game, a player must say, "Adjust," *before* touching any of the pieces.
5. If a player wants to offer the opponent a draw, that player should make his or her next move and then say to the opponent, "I offer you a draw."

Courtesies

1. Players and opponents should shake hands before and after each chess game.
2. During a game, a player should say, "Check," when checking the opponent's King.
3. Players should remain quiet during a chess game.
4. Spectators of a game should not **kibitz**–talk about the game–within the hearing range of either of the players.

Activity 42

⇨ Write **R** before each example of a rule below. Write **C** before each courtesy.

_____ 1. Manuel says, "Check," when he places Jason's King in check.

_____ 2. On her move, Esther touches her Knight and realizes she must move it.

_____ 3. Shauna, playing White, makes the first move in her game with Ivan.

_____ 4. After their game, Daniel and Lynn shake hands.

_____ 5. Ji Xian makes his next move and then offers Stacey a draw.

Answer Key

Activity 1

a. How many squares are on a chessboard? — **64**

b. How many squares are along each side of a chessboard? — **8**

c. At the beginning of a game, what color square (*white* or *black*) should be at the lower right-hand corner of the chessboard? — **white**

d. At the beginning of a game, what color square (*white* or *black*) should be at the lower left-hand corner of the chessboard? — **black**

e. Does a chessboard contain more *light* squares, more *dark* squares, or an *equal* number of light and dark squares? — **equal**

Activity 2

a. How many ranks does a chessboard contain? — **8**

b. How many files does a chessboard contain? — **8**

c. How many squares are on the longest diagonal of a chessboard? — **8**

d. A *file* runs **up and down**, and a *rank* runs **left to right**.

e. Match each chess term on the left with its definition on the right.

Chess Terms	Definitions
b 1. rank	a) slanted line
c 2. file	b) row
a 3. diagonal	c) column

Activity 3

a. How many pieces does each player have when play begins? — **16**

b. How many pieces are on the chessboard when play begins? — **32**

c. In the diagram below, write the names of the circled pieces.

Rook, Pawn, Queen, King, Bishop, Knight

Activity 4

a. In the starting position, on what color squares are the Queens placed?

white Queen? **white**   black Queen? **black**

b. In the starting position, on what color squares are the Kings placed?

white King? **black**   black King? **white**

c. On the diagram at right, show the starting positions of both white and black pieces. Use the following abbreviations: K = King, Q = Queen, R = Rook, B = Bishop, N = Knight, and P = pawn.

d. On your completed diagram, draw a circle around each Queen.

e. On your completed diagram, draw a square around each Rook.

Activity 5

Use the diagram at right to do the following:

a. Write an **X** on each square to which the black King can move on its next move.

b. Write an **X** on each square to which the white King can move on its next move.

c. What is the least number of moves in which the white King can move to the black square in the lower left-hand corner of the board? — **7**

d. What is the least number of moves in which the white King can move to the white square in the upper left-hand corner of the board? — **7**

Activity 6

Follow the instructions for each diagram below.

a. Circle and name the pieces that the black King can capture:

Bishop and **Rook**

b. Circle and name the pieces that the white King can capture:

Knight and **Pawn**

Activity 7

Use the diagram at right to do the following:

a. Write an **X** on each square to which the black Queen can move, and circle any piece the black Queen can capture.

b. Draw a circle on each square the black Queen cannot reach because its movement is blocked by other pieces.

c. Name the piece that is blocking the Queen's free movement along one of her two diagonals. — **Knight**

Activity 8

Follow the instructions for each diagram below.

a. Write an **X** on each square to which the white Queen can move, and circle any piece the white Queen can capture.

b. Write an **X** on each square to which the black Queen can move, and circle any piece the black Queen can capture.

Answer Key

Activity 9

⇨ Use the diagram at right to do the following:

a. Write an **X** on each square to which the white Rook can move, and circle any piece the white Rook can capture.

b. Draw a circle on each square the white Rook cannot reach because its movement is blocked by other pieces.

Activity 10

⇨ Follow the instructions for each diagram below.

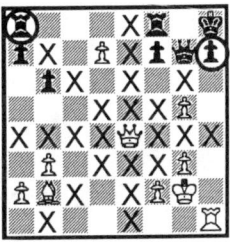 

a. Write an **X** on each square to which the white Queen can move, and circle any piece the white Queen can capture.

b. Write an **X** on each square to which the black Queen can move, and circle any piece the black Queen can capture.

c. Write an **X** on each square to which the black Rook can move, and circle any piece the black Rook can capture.

d. Write an **X** on each square to which the white Rook can move, and circle any piece the white Rook can capture.

Activity 11

⇨ Use the diagram at right to do the following:

a. Write an **X** on each square to which the white Bishop can move.

b. Circle the piece that the white Bishop can capture.

c. On what color squares (*white* or *black*) must the white Bishop stay throughout the game?   __black__
   (*white* or *black*?)

Activity 12

⇨ Use the diagram at right to do the following:

a. Write an **X** on each square to which the white Knight can move.

b. Circle the pieces that the white Knight can capture.

c. Suppose the white Knight makes three moves from its present position. On what color square will it land?   __white__
   (*white* or *black*?)

Activity 13

⇨ Follow the instructions for each diagram below.

a. Write an **X** on each square to which the white Bishop can move, and circle any piece the white Bishop can capture.

b. Write an **X** on each square to which the black Bishop can move, and circle any piece the black Bishop can capture.

 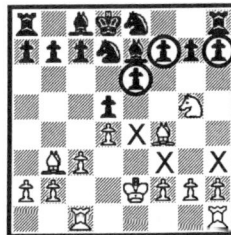

c. Write an **X** on each square to which the black Knight can move, and circle any piece the black Knight can capture.

d. Write an **X** on each square to which the white Knight can move, and circle any piece the white Knight can capture.

Activity 14

⇨ Use the diagram to the right to do the following:

a. Write an **X** on each square to which a white pawn can move.

b. Circle any piece that a white pawn can capture.

c. Draw a square around the only white pawn that can move two squares on its next move.

Answer Key

Activity 15

➪ On the diagram at right, Black just made the pawn move indicated by the arrow. It is now White's move.

  a. Draw an arrow to the square where the white pawn moves in order to capture *en passant*.

  b. Circle the black pawn that the white pawn may capture.

Activity 18

➪ Use the diagram at right to do the following:

  a. Circle the white piece that is checking the black King.

  b. Write an **X** on the flight square to which the black King can move.

Activity 16

➪ a. When a pawn is promoted to the eighth rank, what type of piece may it become?

  Queen   Rook   Bishop   Knight

  b. On the diagram at right, circle the white pawn that can be promoted to a Queen on its next move. *Remember, on a chess diagram, the white pawns move from the bottom to the top; black pawns move from top to bottom.*

  c. On the diagram at right, circle the black pawn that can be promoted to a Queen on its next move.

Activity 19

➪ Draw an arrow on each diagram below to show the checking move.

  a. Black to move the Queen and check the white King.

Black to move.

  b. White to move the Rook and check the black King.

White to move.

  c. White to move the Bishop and check the black King.

White to move.

  d. Black to move the Knight and check the white King.

Black to move.

Activity 17

➪ Follow the instructions for each diagram below.

  a. Circle each pawn that can move two squares on its next move.

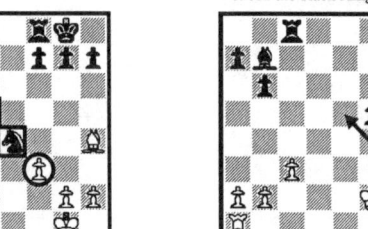

  b. Circle each pawn that can capture an opponent's piece on its next move. Draw a square around each threatened piece.

  c. Black just made the pawn move indicated by the arrow. Draw an arrow to the square where a white pawn can move to make an *en passant* capture. Circle the black pawn that will be captured.

  d. Circle each pawn that can be promoted to a Queen on its next move.

Activity 20

➪ In each diagram below, explain why the white King cannot move to the circled square: *cannot remain in check* or *cannot move into check*.

a. __cannot move into check__

b. __cannot remain in check__

Answer Key

Activity 21

➪ In each diagram, explain why the black King cannot move to the circled square: *cannot capture a guarded piece* or *cannot move next to the opponent's King*.

a. __cannot move next to the opponent's King__

b. __cannot capture a guarded piece__

Activity 22

➪ a. Below each diagram, circle how Black can get out of check: *flee, interpose,* or *capture*.

b. Draw an arrow on each diagram to show the move that gets the black King out of check. Circle any captured piece.

(**Flee?**) Interpose? Capture?   Flee? (**Interpose?**) Capture?

 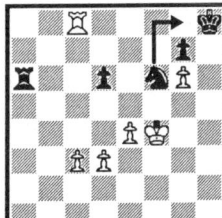

Flee? Interpose? (**Capture?**)   Flee? (**Interpose?**) Capture?

Activity 23

➪ Use the diagram at the right to complete the following:

a. Black can castle __King-side__.
   (King-side or *Queen-side?)*

b. White can castle __Queen-side__.
   (King-side or *Queen-side?)*

c. Write a **K** on the square where each King lands after castling, and an **R** where each Rook lands.

d. During a game, how many times can each King castle? __1__
   number

Activity 24

➪ Answer the two questions beside each diagram below.

a. Why can't Black castle King-side on the next move?
__Black's King would pass through check.__

b. Why can't White castle at all this game?
__White's King has already moved.__

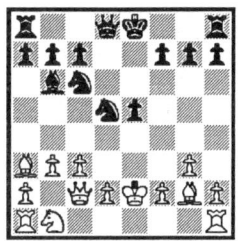

c. Why can't White castle on the next move?
__White is in check.__

d. Why can't Black castle King-side on the next move?
__The Knight is between the King and Rook.__

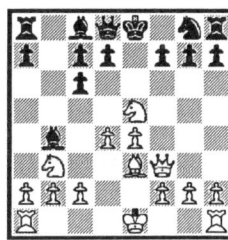

Activity 25

➪ Use the diagram at right to do the following:

a. Circle the white piece that is checkmating the black King.

b. Name the checkmating piece: __Queen__

c. Why can't the black King capture the Queen?
__The Queen is guarded by the white Bishop.__

Activity 26

➪ Draw an arrow on each diagram below to show the checkmating Queen move. Circle any captured piece that results in checkmate.

a. White to move the Queen and checkmate in one move.

b. Black to move the Queen and checkmate in one move.

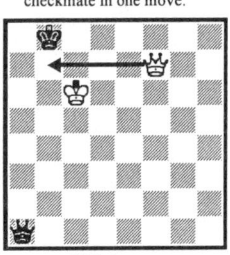 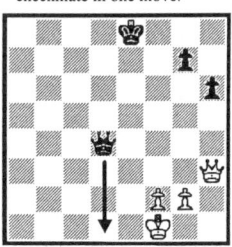

White to move. Black to move.

c. White to move the Queen and checkmate in one move.

d. Black to move the Queen and checkmate in one move.

 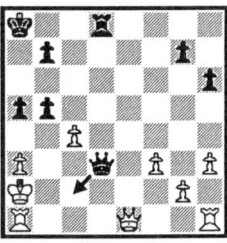

White to move. Black to move.

Answer Key

Activity 27

➪ Draw an arrow on each diagram below to show the checkmating Rook move.

a. Black to move the Rook and checkmate in one move.

Black to move.

b. White to move the Rook and checkmate in one move.

White to move.

c. Black to move a Rook and checkmate in one move.

Black to move.

d. White to move the Rook and checkmate in one move.

White to move.

Activity 28

➪ Draw an arrow on each diagram below to show the checkmating move.

a. White to move the Bishop and checkmate in one move.

White to move.

b. Black to move the Knight and checkmate in one move.

Black to move.

c. White to move the Bishop and checkmate in one move.

White to move.

d. Black to move a pawn and checkmate in one move.

Black to move.

Activity 29

➪ The two games below are over. Under each diagram, circle how the game ended: *stalemate draw* or *checkmate*.

Stalemate Draw?   (Checkmate?)   (Stalemate Draw?)   Checkmate?

Activity 30

a. In the diagram at right, the game ended in a draw. Explain why.

There is a lack of checkmating material.

b. Name the type of draw that occurs when one player puts the other player's King in an endless series of checks.

perpetual check

Activity 31

a. In the diagram at right, what will be the result of the game if it is White's move and White promotes the pawn to a Queen?

The game will end as a stalemate draw.

b. In the diagram at right, should Black promote the pawn to a Queen, Rook, Bishop, or Knight? Give a reason for your answer.

Black should promote to a Knight because it checkmates White.

Activity 32

➪ Match each combination of pieces on the left with the combination of pieces on the right that has the same point value.

_d_ 1. ♞♞   a) ♛
_e_ 2. ♞   b) ♝♙♙
_a_ 3. ♜♝♙   c) ♜♜
_b_ 4. ♜   d) ♜♙
_c_ 5. ♛♙   e) ♙♙♙

Answer Key

Activity 33

The activity below will challenge your ability to find a checkmating move. Your goal is to find the correct move in each diagram. You decide which piece to move and where to move it! Good luck!

⇨ Draw an arrow on each diagram below to show the checkmating move.

a. White to move and checkmate in one move.

White to move.

b. Black to move and checkmate in one move.

Black to move.

c. White to move and checkmate in one move.

White to move.

d. Black to move and checkmate in one move.

Black to move.

Notice that White cannot use the Bishop to take the Knight. Moving the Bishop would put the white King in check from the black Queen! The Bishop is said to be "pinned" to the King.

Activity 34

In this activity, you are to find a move that *prevents checkmate*! For example, in diagram **a**, you find a move for Black that prevents White from checkmating Black on White's next move.

⇨ Draw an arrow on each diagram to show a move that protects against checkmate.

a. Black to move and prevent White from checkmating.

Black to move.

b. White to move and prevent Black from checkmating.

White to move.

c. Black to move and prevent White from checkmating.

Black to move.

d. White to move and prevent Black from checkmating.

White to move.

Activity 35

⇨ Using the board at right, write the name of the square on which each piece is sitting.

black King: **g8**
white King: **e3**
black pawn: **f5**
white pawn: **d3**
black Queen: **c6**
white Rook: **d1**

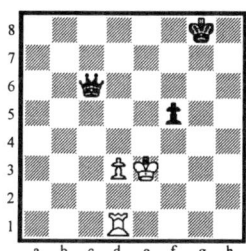

Activity 36

⇨ On the board at right, piece moves are shown by arrows. Record each move in algebraic notation

white pawn: **h3**   black pawn: **b5**
white Knight: **Nf3**   black Bishop: **Bc4**
white Queen: **Qa3**   black Rook: **Rd8**
white King: **Kh1**   black Queen: **Qd6**

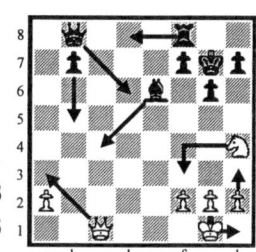

Activity 37

⇨ Write the move indicated by the arrow on each diagram. For each move, use one or more of the symbols (×, +, #, 0-0, 0-0-0) as needed.

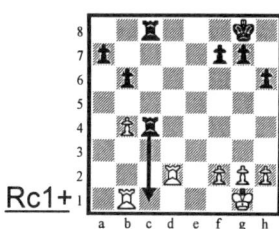
Rc1+

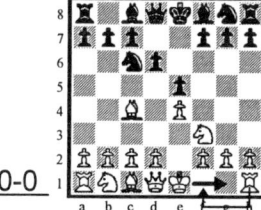
0-0

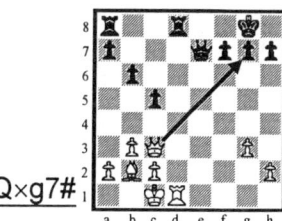
Q×g7#

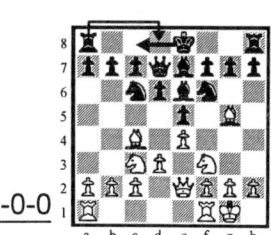
0-0-0

Activity 38

⇨ Looking at the board at right, how would you record the following moves?

a. White uses the Rook on a8 to capture the black Queen. **R8×a5**
b. White uses the Rook on a3 to capture the black Queen. **R3×a5**
c. Black uses the Knight on f5 to capture the white Bishop. **Nf×e3**
d. Black uses the Knight on g4 to capture the white Bishop. **Ng×e3**

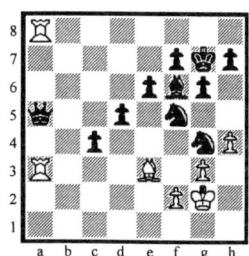

Answer Key

Activity 39

➩ On the board at right, each player has made 5 moves of a second King pawn opening. The first 4 moves are listed below.

Fill in the blank lines to show each player's 5th move.

	White	Black
1.	e4	e5
2.	Nf3	Nc6
3.	d3	Nf6
4.	Bg5	Be7
5.	**g3**	**0-0**

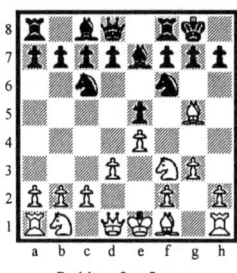

Position after 5 moves.

Activity 40

➩ On the board at right, each player has made 5 moves of a second Queen pawn opening. The first 4 moves are listed below.

Fill in the blank lines to show each player's 5th move.

	White	Black
1.	d4	Nf6
2.	c4	e6
3.	Nf3	Bb4+
4.	Nc3	Bxc3+
5.	**bxc3**	**0-0**

Position after 5 moves.

Activity 41

➩ Write the move indicated by the arrow on each diagram. Following the move, write the symbol (!, ?, ??, e.p., or = Q) that best describes the move.

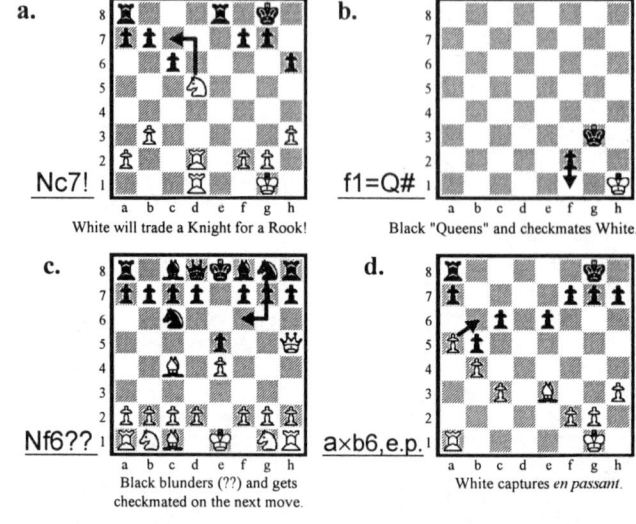

a. **Nc7!**
White will trade a Knight for a Rook!

b. **f1=Q#**
Black "Queens" and checkmates White.

c. **Nf6??**
Black blunders (??) and gets checkmated on the next move.

d. **axb6, e.p.**
White captures *en passant*.

Activity 42

➩ Write **R** before each example of a rule below. Write **C** before each courtesy.

C 1. Manuel says, "Check," when he places Jason's King in check.

R 2. On her move, Esther touches her Knight and realizes she must move it.

R 3. Shauna, playing White, makes the first move in her game with Ivan.

C 4. After their game, Daniel and Lynn shake hands.

R 5. Ji Xian makes his next move before offering Stacey a draw.

Learning Plus is pleased to bring you this fine chess product. Students who are familiar with chess rules and chess play may be interested in the next-level book, *Chess Tactics For Students*, also by John Bain. *Chess Tactics For Students* is available from your favorite chess materials distributor, or you may contact the publisher directly by mail or phone at the address given below.

Learning Plus
P.O. Box 713
Corvallis, Oregon 97339-0713
(541) 757-7049